The College Experience Compact

Second Edition

The College Experience Compact

Amy Baldwin
University of Central Arkansas

Brian Tietje
California Polytechnic State University

Paul G. Stoltz
Peak Learning

PEARSON

Boston   Columbus   Hoboken   Indianapolis   New York   San Francisco
Amsterdam   Cape Town   Dubai   London   Madrid   Milan   Munich   Paris   Montréal   Toronto
Delhi   Mexico City   São Paulo   Sydney   Hong Kong   Seoul   Singapore   Taipei   Tokyo

VP Student Success & Career Development: Jodi McPherson
Program Manager: Anne Shure
Senior Development Editor: Elana Dolberg
Executive Marketing Manager: Amy Judd
Senior Media Producer: Tracy Cunningham
Senior Development Editor: Charlotte Morrissey
Associate Content Specialist: Celeste Kmiotek
Project Manager: Rebecca Gilpin
Project Coordination and Text Design: MPS North America LLC

Electronic Page Makeup: Laserwords Private Ltd
Associate Director of Design: Andrea Nix
Program Design Lead: Beth Paquin
Cover Design: MPS North America LLC
Cover Image: Duncan1890/Getty Images
Interior Design Images: Lusikkolbaskin/Fotolia, Rawpixel/Fotolia
Senior Manufacturing Buyer: Roy L. Pickering, Jr.
Printer/Binder: Courier/Kendallville
Cover Printer: Courier/Kendallville

Credits and acknowledgments borrowed from other sources and reproduced, with permission, in this textbook appear on appropriate page within text.

Library of Congress Cataloging-in-Publication Data
Baldwin, Amy, date-
    The college experience compact / Amy Baldwin, University of Central Arkansas Brian Tietje,
California Polytechnic State University, Paul G. Stoltz, Peak Learning. — Second edition.
    pages cm
Includes bibliographical references and index.
ISBN 978-0-321-98002-1
1. College student orientation—United States. 2. College students—Conduct of life.
I. Tietje, Brian C. II. Stoltz, Paul G. III. Title.
LB2343.32.B2384 2016
378.1'98—dc23
                                                                2014040905

10 9 8 7 6 5 4 3 2—V011—17 16 15

PEARSON

www.pearsonhighered.com

Student Edition ISBN 10:   0-321-98002-6
Student Edition ISBN 13: 978-0-321-98002-1
A la Carte ISBN 10:   0-13-403879-7
A la Carte ISBN 13:   978-0-13-403879-7

About the Authors

AMY BALDWIN, MA, is a pioneering educator and educational entrepreneur. She wrote the first, groundbreaking student success textbook for community colleges and for first-generation students. In response to nationwide demand, in 2011 she founded Educational Frontiers Group (EFG), which provides educational services such as consulting, professional development, and educational novelties. As a result of her work with national initiatives such as Complete College America, Achieving the Dream, and the Developmental Education Initiative, she has become one of the most sought-after keynote speakers and workshop facilitators on student success and engagement topics. After 18 years as a community college professor at Pulaski Technical College, where she was awarded the 2006 Susan Faulkner Award for Exceptional Teaching for the Two-Year College English Association Southwest Chapter, she now serves as director of University College at the University of Central Arkansas. She has gained considerable acclaim for her efforts toward helping students get in, get through, get out, and get paid.

BRIAN TIETJE, PhD, is a thought leader in higher education and a passionate advocate for student success, particularly for students who face challenging circumstances and who aren't familiar with the unwritten rules of college and career success. Brian took his life experiences and determination from rural Ohio cross-country as he traversed educational and corporate ladders to reach an executive leadership position in higher education. He presently serves as vice provost of International, Graduate, and Extended Education at Cal Poly State University, and serves on the board of directors of several private and not-for-profit organizations. He is continually pursuing opportunities for educational innovation to meet the needs of students and employers. Prior to his administrative leadership career, Brian was awarded the Orfalea College of Business Distinguished Teacher Award in 2000 and 2001 at Cal Poly, and the Most Outstanding Marketing Faculty award in 2002, 2003, and 2004, also at Cal Poly.

PAUL G. STOLTZ, PhD, is a *New York Times* number 1 bestselling author and considered the world's foremost authority on the science and method of measuring and strengthening GRIT™, also known as "GRIT 2.0." His methods and teachings are used at Harvard, MIT, Cornell, Stanford, Carnegie Mellon, and by top organizations in 63 countries. Paul has been selected as one of the Top Ten Most Influential Global Thinkers by *HR Magazine,* one of the Top 100 Thinkers of Our Time by *Executive Excellence,* and the Millennial Thought Leader in Singapore. He's the originator of the globally acclaimed AQ® (Adversity Quotient®) method, adopted worldwide, and has written four bestselling books on the subject—published by Wiley, Harper-Collins, Simon & Schuster, and Penguin—in 17 languages. Paul has been featured in much of the world's top media, including *Fortune, Forbes, Success, Business Week, Financial Times, Wall Street Journal, Asia 21,* Fox, ABC Nightly News, NBC, CBS, *The Today Show,* and multiple appearances on *The Oprah Show.* He is the founding director of the GRIT Institute and the Global Resilience Institute, conducting research in 29 countries, as well as founder and CEO of PEAK Learning, Inc., the global research and consulting firm he formed in 1987. Applying his vast experience and research in higher education specifically to students in their first year of college is a long-term goal of his. Developing effective strategies toward college completion—and sustainable employment—has never been timelier.

Brief Contents

Contents

viii CONTENTS

Acknowledgments

Amy Baldwin

To my family, Kyle, Emily, and Will: Thank you for your continued support and patience.
To my Pearson family, Jodi McPherson, Katie Mahan, Elana Dolberg, Amy Judd, and all those who have provided feedback and creative ideas: Thank you for your hard work and your friendship.

Brian Tietje

I thank God for Debbie, my awesome wife who encourages and inspires me; Amy and Paul, the best (and grittiest) coauthors on the planet; and Jodi, Elana, Shannon, and the Pearson team who work so hard to support our success.

Paul G. Stoltz

I thank Ronda, my inspiration and the living exemplar of good, smart, and massive GRIT, my generous coauthors Amy and Brian for welcoming my child (GRIT) into their home (Student Success), Shannon for stepping up and climbing strong, Jodi and the Pearson team for having the vision to equip students with the GRIT it takes to get in, get through, get out, and get paid, the enlightened professors who commit to GRIT, and all the gritty students out there who find a way to dig deep and do whatever it takes to make a positive impact on the world, in spite of whatever gets in their way!

Thanks also from all of us to the reviewers of this edition:

Gabriel Adona, *San Diego Mesa College*
Pamela Bilton Beard, *Houston Community College Southwest*
Mei Mei Burr, *Northern Kentucky University*
Donna Colondres, *Chaffey College*
Lory Conrad, *University of Arkansas–Fort Smith*
Christine Crowe, *Suffolk Community College*
Raven Davenport, *Houston Community College*
Luke E. Faust, *Indiana University of Pennsylvania*
Shirley Flor, *San Diego Mesa College*
Alonzo Flowers, *Blinn College*
Kim Forcier, *University of Texas–San Antonio*
Barry Foster, *Brazosport Community College*
Patricia S. Foster, *Stephen F. Austin State University*
Altheria Gaston Monique Gilchrist, *Community College of Philadelphia*
Mary Gumlia, *Solano Community College*
Linda M. Hensen-Jackson, *Arkansas Tech University*
Lauren Hensley, *The Ohio State University*
Robert Irizarry, *Brazosport College*
Kimberly Koledoye, *Houston Community College Northwest*
Rula Mourad Koudsia, *Ivy Tech Community College Northeast*
Alice Lanning, *University of Oklahoma*
Catherine Lee, *Cape Fear Community College*
Rhonda Lee Meadows, *West Virginia University*

Shannon E. McCasland, *Aims Community College*
Cynthia Pascal, *The Art Institute of Washington*
Melissa Rathburn, *University of South Florida*
Jacqueline Robinson, *Milwaukee Area Technical College*
Amy Skeens, *West Virginia University*
Leigh Smith, *Lamar Institute of Technology*
Ellen Stohl, *California State University–Northridge*
Margaret A. Soucy, *Western New Mexico University*
Victoria Washington, *Houston Community College*
Cornelia Wills, *Middle Tennessee State University*
Jennifer Woltjen, *Broome Community College*

Preface

Your Challenge, Our Promise

Beat the Odds. Graduate Strong!

While many of your students have worked very hard to be in your class this semester and are eager to start their college career, most college students stumble, fall short, or even quit as they strive to *get in, get through, get out, and get paid.* The statistics and trends can seem pretty dismal. That's the bad news.

The Good News

The good news is this book will equip your students to beat the odds. It will give them exactly what they need to not just survive, but to also come out strong.

How? To help them build the necessary skills to complete college successfully, this book provides powerful, proven content and tools through information about what it takes to meet the academic, social, personal, and professional expectations of college.

This book also has a cutting-edge advantage over other student success books: it includes content and applications for GRIT, the capacity to dig deep and do whatever it takes. Research has proven that GRIT is the single most powerful predictor of success. By including GRIT coupled with direct information about the way college works, we'll show what it *really* takes to succeed. That's our promise.

- **GETTING IN** Whether or not your students are truly college ready, they will need help understanding the unwritten rules of transitioning from high school or work to college. *This book provides the basic, no-fluff information that helps students learn how college works.*

- **GETTING THROUGH** Your students need more than just help getting settled into college; they also need to know how to keep going when they hit roadblocks along the way. *This book gives students the tools to overcome the obstacles with resilience and tenacity.*

- **GETTING OUT** Graduating from college with a degree in hand is every student's dream. However, not all students know what it takes to finish college. *This book delivers both content and strategies for reaching long-term goals by showing students the steps to college completion and equipping them with the GRIT it will take to walk across the graduation stage.*

- **GETTING PAID** Your students want to move from college to a career with as few challenges as possible, but they often do not connect the work they are doing in college to the world of work. *This book lays the groundwork for building on professional skills that will lead to career success.*

New to This Edition

This edition is tailored to the one credit or blended/online college experience and framed in a practical, situational way that helps students navigate *what* to do, *when* do it, and *where* to go for support. Aligned with learning outcomes from both MyStudentSuccessLab and Student Success CourseConnect, it is designed as a standalone book or a print companion with one of these technologies.

Develop GRIT

How do students from any background beat the odds, regardless of their advantages or disadvantages in life? Research has proven GRIT is the single most powerful predictor of student success, both in and beyond school. Now available for the first time to the academic market, this book provides the scientifically grounded simple, practical, proven tips and tools students need to grow greater GRIT.

- **GRIT Tips** are quick, practical tips to effectively apply all four dimensions of **GRIT** (**G**rowth, **R**esilience, **I**nstinct, and **T**enacity) to each of the lessons.
- **GRIT Gainers** are tough, edgy, inspirational applications related to each section.
- **How Gritty Are You?** is a "get real" moment for students to assess and amplify their motivation and mindset to put the chapter's lessons to work.
- **Putting It in Practice: The GRIT Advantage** equips and compels students to put the chapter's tools into practice.

Getting In

College acceptance rates have dropped, making it harder for students to get in. In 2014, Stanford University had an acceptance rate of 5.7%! And getting into college is just the first step. This book provides students who beat these odds with a firm foundation of GRIT-based, scientifically grounded tools and skills necessary to be successful.

Getting Through

Only 55 percent of students in two-year public schools returned in the second year. Students in four-year public schools performed a bit better (64.9%), but over a third of freshmen did not return as sophomores. This book provides students with strategies to develop a gritty mindset and skillset to get through college.

- **The Unwritten Rules** let students know what college is really like, as the feature shares the secrets to college success by telling them what usually takes years to figure out on their own.
- **It's in the Syllabus** reminds students to review one of the most important documents in college—the "contract" between their instructors and themselves—by asking them a few questions about the document. Knowing how to use the syllabus will help students get through college.
- **Integrity Matters** provides students the opportunity to think critically about strengthening their integrity with real-life college situations, as acting with integrity is a big part of getting through.
- **Opening stories** run throughout the book and present four characters on their journey as first-time college students. The stories provide opportunities for your students to relate to their situations and end-of-story questions that help students think about the challenges they face and what choices they can make.

Getting Out

Only 26.5 percent of students who had started at a two-year public school had completed their degree after six years, and only 10 percent of those students had completed their degree at a four-year institution. This book provides the first-ever blend of the gritty skillset and mindset needed to graduate.

Getting Paid

Forty-six schools on the 2013 Payscale College ROI report had a negative 20-year net ROI, meaning the costs of attending these schools outweigh the financial benefit. This book equips students with the practical skillset and GRIT-based mindset that global research reveals is what employers crave most.

- **In-chapter and end-of-chapter exercises,** as noted in the previous section above, also reinforce getting out and getting paid.
- **A career planning lesson** offers students the opportunity to apply all that has been learned in order to prepare for the next steps toward life and career planning and set goals for achieving them.

MyStudentSuccessLab™

This title is also available with MyStudentSuccessLab—an online homework, tutorial, and assessment program designed to work with this text to engage students and improve results. Within its structured environment, students practice what they learn, test their understanding, and pursue a plan that helps them better absorb course material and understand difficult concepts.

Personalize Learning with MyStudentSuccessLab

This learning outcomes-based technology promotes student engagement through the following:

- **Full course pre- and post-diagnostic tests** based on Bloom's taxonomy are linked to key learning objectives in each topic.
- Each individual topic in the Learning Path offers a **pre- and post-test** dedicated to that topic, an **overview** of objectives to build vocabulary and repetition, access to **video interviews** to learn about key issues "by students, for students," **practice exercises** to improve class prep and learning, and **graded activities** to build critical thinking skills and develop problem solving abilities.
- **Student resources** include Finish Strong 247 YouTube videos, calculators, and professionalism/research and writing/student success tools.
- **Student inventories** increase self-awareness and include Golden Personality (similar to Myers-Briggs and gives insights on personal style) and Conley Readiness Index (CRI) (measures readiness and likelihood for success and gives insight into student aspirations).
- A **title-specific version** is available as an option for those who teach closely to their text. This course would include the national eText, chapter-specific quizzing, and Learning Path modules that align with the chapter naming conventions of the book. Also included are the Experience Series audience-specific booklets *Adult Learners, International Learners, Men of Color,* and *Student Athletes.*

Student Success CourseConnect is one of many award-winning CourseConnect customizable online courses designed by subject-matter experts and credentialed instructional designers. This topical-based technology promotes student engagement and includes the following:

- Library of rich media (audio/video)
- Compatibility with many learning management systems (LMS)

- Flexible discussion questions, syllabi, and assessment content
- iPad-compatible lessons
- Instructor Resource Guide to support facilitation in the online environment
- Option to add ebook
- Online tutorial support
- Analytics Edition available in Pearson Learning Studio platform

Version Overview

You and Your Students Have Unique Needs

Experience books have changed to fulfill your unique needs. The *Experience* books recognize how student and instructor needs have evolved, and have made the change from editions that catered to all institutions to specific programs. In learning environments, it is important to get relevant information at the time you need it. Now you can select course materials from *Experience* that reinforce your institution's culture (four-year, two-year, or one credit hour and/or blended and online) and speak directly to your specific needs.

The Choice Is Yours

Experience combines student success skills with the world's leading method for growing greater GRIT (Growth, Resilience, Instinct, and Tenacity). With a focus on student experience specific to institution type, the *Experience* series for college students incorporates the GRIT framework, supplying learners with powerful success strategies and tools for college completion and career success—*get in, get through, get out,* and *get paid.* The authors recognize that understanding what it takes to succeed in college is one thing, but having the personal GRIT to make it happen is what makes the difference. Framed in a practical, situational manner, the book helps students navigate *what* to do, *when* to do it, and *where* to go for support. It provides scientifically grounded yet practical tips and tools students need to grow greater GRIT, which research shows as the most powerful predictor of success in school and beyond. Students "get in and get through" using a firm foundation of distinctive features to stay in and get through college with academic, social, and transitional skills. In order to "get out and get paid," students are equipped with a blend of professional and GRIT-based mindsets required to successfully graduate and enter a career that fulfills their educational and personal goals.

Choose the version of *Experience* that aligns best with your institution and student population, all while getting the hallmark features and content you've come to expect.

- *The College Experience,* second edition. Written for students attending four-year programs, it addresses today's university and college students.
- *The Community College Experience,* fourth edition. Written for students attending two-year programs, it addresses students in community, technical, and career colleges.
- *The College Experience Compact,* second edition. Written for one credit hour student success courses and/or those with blended and online students, it addresses the needs and challenges of students as digital learners. It aligns with learning outcomes from both the MyStudentSuccessLab (www.mystudentsuccesslab.com), and Student Success CourseConnect online course (www.pearsonlearningsolutions.com/courseconnect). This book is designed for use as a standalone text or a print companion with one of these technologies for blended, online, or one credit hour student success courses.

Instructor Resources

Online Instructor's Manual

(www.pearsonhighered.com/irc)

This manual provides a framework of ideas and suggestions for activities, journal writing, thought-provoking situations, and online implementation, including MyStudentSuccessLab recommendations.

Online PowerPoint Presentation

(www.pearsonhighered.com/irc)

This comprehensive set of PowerPoint slides can be used by instructors for class presentations and also by students for lecture preview or review. The PowerPoint presentation includes summary slides with overview information for each chapter to help students understand and review concepts within each chapter.

MyStudentSuccessLab

(www.mystudentsuccesslab.com)

This title is also available with MyStudentSuccessLab—an online homework, tutorial, and assessment program designed to work with this text to engage students and improve results. Within its structured environment, students practice what they learn, test their understanding, and pursue a plan that helps them better absorb course material and understand difficult concepts. Beyond the full course pre- and post-diagnostic assessments and pre- and post-tests within each module, additional learning outcomes-based tests can be created/selected using a secure testing engine and may be printed or delivered online. If you are interested in adopting this title with MyStudentSuccessLab, ask your Pearson representative for the correct package ISBN and course to download.

Course Redesign

(www.pearsoncourseredesign.com)

Collect, measure, and interpret data to support efficacy. Our resources can help you rethink how you deliver instruction, measure the results of your course redesign, and get support for data collection and interpretation.

Implementation and Training

(www.mystudentsuccesscommunity.com)

Access MyStudentSuccessLab training resources such as the Best Practices implementation guide, How Do I videos, self-paced training modules, 1:1 Expert on Demand sessions with a faculty advisor, and videos, posts, and communication from student success peers.

CourseConnect

(www.pearsonlearningsolutions.com/courseconnect)

This title is also available with CourseConnect—designed by subject-matter experts and credentialed instructional designers, it offers customizable online courses with a consistent learning path, available in a variety of learning management systems as self-paced study.

CourseSmart Textbooks Online

(www.coursesmart.com)

As an alternative to purchasing the print textbook, students can subscribe to the same content online and save up to 50 percent off the suggested list price of the print text. With a CourseSmart eTextbook, students can search the text, make notes online, print out reading assignments that incorporate lecture notes, and bookmark important passages for review.

Custom Services

(www.pearsonlearningsolutions.com)

With this title, we offer flexible and creative choices for course materials that will maximize learning and student engagement. Options include custom library, publications, technology solutions, and online education.

Professional Development for Instructors

(www.pearsonhighered.com/studentsuccess)

Augment your teaching with engaging resources. Visit our online catalog for our Ownership series, Engaging Activities series, and Audience booklets.

Resources for Your Students

(www.pearsonhighered.com/studentsuccess)

Help students save and succeed throughout their college experience. Visit our online catalog for options such as Books à la Carte, CourseSmart eTextbooks, Pearson Students program, IDentity Series, Success Tips, and more.

Pearson Course Redesign
Collect, measure, and interpret data to support efficacy.

Rethink the way you deliver instruction.

Pearson has successfully partnered with colleges and universities engaged in course redesign for over 10 years through workshops, Faculty Advisor programs, and online conferences. Here's how to get started!

- Visit our course redesign site at www.pearsoncourseredesign.com for information on getting started, a list of Pearson-sponsored course redesign events, and recordings of past course redesign events.

- Request to connect with a Faculty Advisor, a fellow instructor who is an expert in course redesign, by visiting www.mystudentsuccesslab.com/community.

- Join our Course Redesign Community at www.community.pearson.com/courseredesign and connect with colleagues around the country who are participating in course redesign projects.

Don't forget to measure the results of your course redesign!

Examples of data you may want to collect include:

- Improvement of homework grades, test averages, and pass rates over past semesters

- Correlation between time spent in an online product and final average in the course

- Success rate in the next level of the course

- Retention rate (i.e., percentage of students who drop, fail, or withdraw)

Need support for data collection and interpretation?

Ask your local Pearson representative how to connect with a member of Pearson's Efficacy Team.

MyStudentSuccessLab

Help students start strong and finish stronger.

MyStudentSuccessLab™

MyLab from Pearson has been designed and refined with a single purpose in mind—to help educators break through to improving results for their students.

MyStudentSuccessLab™ (MSSL) is a learning outcomes-based technology that advances students' knowledge and builds critical skills, offering ongoing personal and professional development through peer-led video interviews, interactive practice exercises, and activities that focus on academic, life, and professional preparation.

The **Conley Readiness Index (CRI), developed by Dr. David Conley, is now embedded in MyStudentSuccessLab.** This research-based, self-diagnostic online tool measures college and career readiness; it is personalized, research-based, and provides actionable data. Dr. David Conley is a nationally recognized leader in research, policy, and solution development with a sincere passion for improving college and career readiness.

Developed exclusively for Pearson by Dr. Conley, the Conley Readiness Index assesses mastery in each of the "Four Keys" that are critical to college and career readiness:

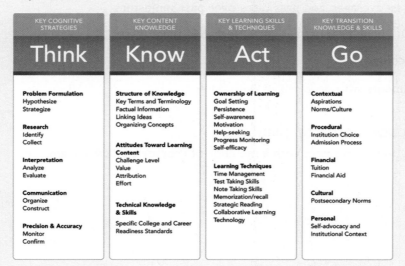

KEY COGNITIVE STRATEGIES	KEY CONTENT KNOWLEDGE	KEY LEARNING SKILLS & TECHNIQUES	KEY TRANSITION KNOWLEDGE & SKILLS
Think	**Know**	**Act**	**Go**
Problem Formulation Hypothesize Strategize **Research** Identify Collect **Interpretation** Analyze Evaluate **Communication** Organize Construct **Precision & Accuracy** Monitor Confirm	**Structure of Knowledge** Key Terms and Terminology Factual Information Linking Ideas Organizing Concepts **Attitudes Toward Learning Content** Challenge Level Value Attribution Effort **Technical Knowledge & Skills** Specific College and Career Readiness Standards	**Ownership of Learning** Goal Setting Persistence Self-awareness Motivation Help-seeking Progress Monitoring Self-efficacy **Learning Techniques** Time Management Test Taking Skills Note Taking Skills Memorization/recall Strategic Reading Collaborative Learning Technology	**Contextual** Aspirations Norms/Culture **Procedural** Institution Choice Admission Process **Financial** Tuition Financial Aid **Cultural** Postsecondary Norms **Personal** Self-advocacy and Institutional Context

Topics include:

Student Success Learning Path

- Conley Readiness Index
- College Transition
- Communication
- Creating an Academic Plan
- Critical Thinking
- Financial Literacy
- Goal Setting
- Information Literacy
- Learning Preferences
- Listening and Note Taking
- Majors and Careers Exploration
- Memory and Studying
- Online Learning
- Problem Solving
- Reading and Annotating
- Stress Management
- Test Taking
- Time Management

Career Success Learning Path

- Career Portfolio
- Interviewing
- Job Search
- Self-Management Skills at Work
- Teamwork
- Workplace Communication
- Workplace Etiquette

www.mystudentsuccesslab.com

Assessment

Beyond the Pre- and Post-Full Course Diagnostic Assessments and Pre- and Post-Tests within each module, additional learning-outcome-based tests can be created using a secure testing engine, and may be printed or delivered online. These tests can be customized by editing individual questions or entire tests.

Reporting

Measurement matters—and is ongoing in nature. MyStudentSuccessLab lets you determine what data you need, set up your course accordingly, and collect data via reports. The high quality and volume of test questions allows for data comparison and measurement.

Content and Functionality Training

The Instructor Implementation Guide provides grading rubrics, suggestions for video use, and more to save time on course prep. Our Best Practices Guide and "How do I…" YouTube videos indicate how to use MyStudentSuccessLab, from getting started to utilizing the Gradebook.

Peer Support

The Student Success Community site is a place for you to connect with other educators to exchange ideas and advice on courses, content, and MyStudentSuccessLab. The site is filled with timely articles, discussions, video posts, and more. Join, share, and be inspired!
www.mystudentsuccesscommunity.com

The Faculty Advisor Network is Pearson's peer-to-peer mentoring program in which experienced MyStudentSuccessLab users share best practices and expertise. Our Faculty Advisors are experienced in one-on-one phone and email coaching, presentations, and live training sessions.

Integration and Compliance

You can integrate our digital solutions with your learning management system in a variety of ways. For more information, or if documentation is needed for ADA compliance, contact your local Pearson representative.

MyStudentSuccessLab users have access to:

- Full course Pre- and Post-Diagnostic Assessments linked to learning outcomes

- Pre- and Post-tests dedicated to individual topics

- Overviews that summarize objectives and skills

- Videos on key issues "by students, for students"

- Practice exercises that instill student confidence

- Graded activities to build critical-thinking and problem-solving skills

- Journal writing assignments with online rubrics for consistent, simpler grading

- Resources like Finish Strong 24/7 YouTube videos, calculators, professionalism/research & writing/student success tools

- Student inventories including **Conley Readiness Index** and **Golden Personality**

Students utilizing MyStudentSuccessLab may purchase Pearson texts in a number of cost-saving formats—including eTexts, loose-leaf Books à la Carte editions, and more.

CourseConnect™
Trust that your online course is the best in its class.

Designed by subject matter experts and credentialed instructional designers, CourseConnect offers award-winning customizable online courses that help students build skills for ongoing personal and professional development.

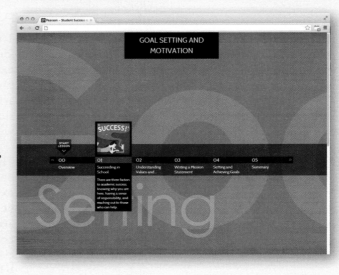

CourseConnect uses topic-based, interactive modules that follow a consistent learning path—from introduction, to presentation, to activity, to review. Its built-in tools—including user-specific pacing charts, personalized study guides, and interactive exercises—provide a student-centric learning experience that minimizes distractions and helps students stay on track and complete the course successfully. Features such as relevant video, audio, and activities, personalized (or editable) syllabi, discussion forum topics and questions, assignments, and quizzes are all easily accessible. CourseConnect is available in a variety of learning management systems and accommodates various term lengths as well as self-paced study. And, our compact textbook editions align to CourseConnect course outcomes.

Choose from the following three course outlines ("Lesson Plans")

Student Success

- Goal Setting, Values, and Motivation
- Time Management
- Financial Literacy
- Creative Thinking, Critical Thinking, and Problem Solving
- Learning Preferences
- Listening and Note-Taking in Class
- Reading and Annotating
- Studying, Memory, and Test-Taking
- Communicating and Teamwork
- Information Literacy
- Staying Balanced: Stress Management
- Career Exploration

Career Success

- Planning Your Career Search
- Knowing Yourself: Explore the Right Career Path
- Knowing the Market: Find Your Career Match
- Preparing Yourself: Gain Skills and Experience Now
- Networking
- Targeting Your Search: Locate Positions, Ready Yourself
- Building a Portfolio: Your Resume and Beyond
- Preparing for Your Interview
- Giving a Great Interview
- Negotiating Job Offers, Ensuring Future Success

Professional Success

- Introducing Professionalism
- Workplace Goal Setting
- Workplace Ethics and Your Career
- Workplace Time Management
- Interpersonal Skills at Work
- Workplace Conflict Management
- Workplace Communications: Email and Presentations
- Effective Workplace Meetings
- Workplace Teams
- Customer Focus and You
- Understanding Human Resources
- Managing Career Growth and Change

Custom Services
Personalize instruction to best facilitate learning.

As the industry leader in custom publishing, we are committed to meeting your instructional needs by offering flexible and creative choices for course materials that will maximize learning and student engagement.

Pearson Custom Library

Using our online book-building system, create a custom book by selecting content from our course-specific collections that consist of chapters from Pearson Student Success and Career Development titles and carefully selected, copyright-cleared, third-party content and pedagogy. www.pearsoncustomlibrary.com

Custom Publications

In partnership with your Pearson representative, modify, adapt, and combine existing Pearson books by choosing content from across the curriculum and organizing it around your learning outcomes. As an alternative, you can work with your Editor to develop your original material and create a textbook that meets your course goals.

Custom Technology Solutions

Work with Pearson's trained professionals, in a truly consultative process, to create engaging learning solutions. From interactive learning tools, to eTexts, to custom websites and portals, we'll help you simplify your life as an instructor.

Online Education

Pearson offers online course content for online classes and hybrid courses. This online content can also be used to enhance traditional classroom courses. Our award-winning CourseConnect includes a fully developed syllabus, media-rich lecture presentations, audio lectures, a wide variety of assessments, discussion board questions, and a strong instructor resource package.

For more information on custom Student Success services, please visit www.pearsonlearningsolutions.com.

The College Experience Compact

1 Your Mission Statement and Goals

Chapter goals to help you
get in, get through, get out, and get paid:

We've adopted the "get in, get through, get out, get paid" theme for this book to describe the different stages of the college experience and the purpose for getting a degree. As you begin your pursuit of a college degree, you will face some important decisions and challenges that will require you to have a clear sense of why you're in college and what you're trying to accomplish.

To meet those goals, this chapter will help you:

- Incorporate three factors to academic success into your life
- Analyze the relationship between values, motivation, and goals for academic success
- Use the characteristics of SMART goals in your own goal setting
- Dig deep, with **GRIT**, and do whatever it takes to fulfill your goals
- Write your mission statement

MyStudentSuccessLab™

Log in to MyStudentSuccessLab.com to deepen your **GRIT** mindset and build the skills you'll need to get through the college experience.

Juanita's Story

© ANDRESR/SHUTTERSTOCK

Juanita calls her mother for the second time in two hours. She just created her schedule, visited with her advisor, and now is looking for where her classes will be. Juanita's mom answers immediately. "Do you think I can do this?"

"Juanita," her mother says, "you always overthink these things. I know you like to be prepared, but things will be different. It's not high school."

The classes seem different from the dual enrollment classes Juanita took in high school.

"Yeah, but it made me nervous when my advisor asked me to choose a degree plan," she replies.

"You did choose electrical engineering, just like we talked about, right?" her mother asks.

"Well, I wanted to talk to you about that. I think I want to go into nursing," Juanita says.

"But you don't like working with people who are sick, Juanita. Besides, engineering is more prestigious," her mother replies. Because of the classes she has taken in her high school's dual enrollment program, Juanita could graduate earlier than her classmates who started this fall, but she knows it will still take a lot of money to do it.

"I will be proud of you whatever you decide, but make a choice and stick with it," her mother says.

Juanita knows her mother is right. She has a goal of getting a degree, but she is not sure how to make the right decisions today.

Now, what do you think?

- How will you handle the added responsibility of making important decisions about your future in college?
  - **a.** Not worry too much; everything will work out
  - **b.** Aim high and "climb strong" even if it requires more work and takes longer
  - **c.** Learn as much as I can about my options by talking to people on campus and attending events geared toward my future
  - **d.** Avoid any major decisions for as long as possible

- What would you do if your plans for the future conflicted with your family's plans for you?
  - **a.** Explain clearly why my plans are better than my family's plans for me
  - **b.** Give serious consideration to my family's ideas about what I should do
  - **c.** Try to get really clear on and stay true to what matters most, no matter what
  - **d.** Do what my family wants me to do; they have supported me and know what is best

Ingredients for Your Success

Congratulations, you've made it to college! Think about the role adversity—difficulties, challenges, hardships, obstacles, limitations—has played in your life so far. Has it been an easy or difficult road? How much GRIT has it taken just to get to where you are today? How deep have you had to dig? How much have you had to struggle, sacrifice, even suffer in order to enroll in college and pursue your dreams? Your journey to this point may not have been easy, but you're here and you're ready to succeed, and we wrote this book because we want to help you. Do you realize that only about 6 percent of the entire world's population has earned a college degree? You have an opportunity to earn a distinction that relatively few people on this planet will achieve, and you deserve a lot of credit for pursuing this noble achievement.

What will it take for you to have success in college? This book is filled with ideas, suggestions, and strategies—the essential skillset and the gritty mindset—to help you succeed. In this chapter, we provide the foundational information you will need to start strong and finish stronger. In this section, however, we've narrowed our list of ingredients for success to three of the most important elements: know why you're here; have a sense of personal responsibility; and connect with others.

Know Why You're Here

A popular approach to problem solving in some organizational circles is what's called "root cause analysis." It describes the effort to uncover the root cause, or primary reason, for a particular outcome or circumstance. One technique for uncovering the root cause of something is to ask "why" five times. Let's start with a simple first question: "Why are you in college?" For example, if your answer to "Why am I in college?" is "I want to get a nursing degree," then the next question is "Why do you want to get a nursing degree?" If your answer to that question is "I want to care for others," ask yourself another why. As you proceed down the path of the 5 Whys, you'll get deeper and deeper into your true motivations for pursuing a college degree, and you'll have a much clearer understanding of yourself and why you are here in college. Here is an example of the how the 5 Whys work.

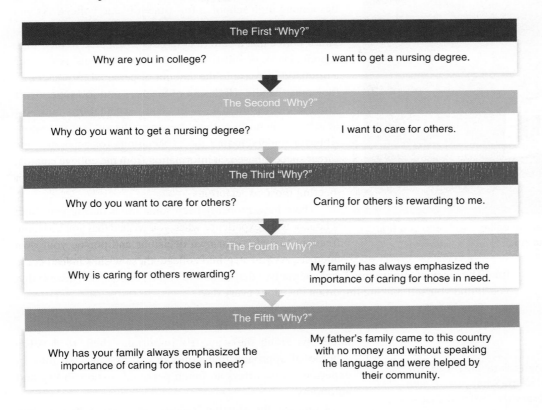

Take a moment to complete Activity 1.1, the Five Whys.

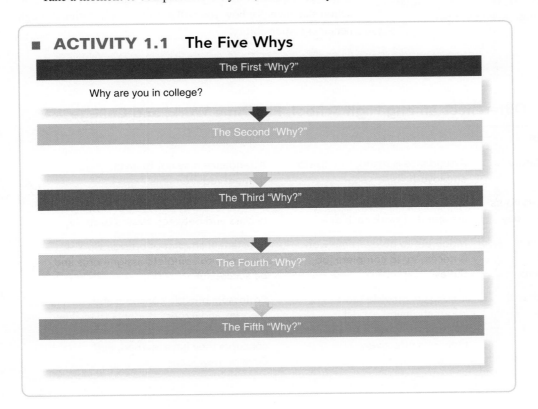

Knowing why you are in college will help you figure out where you want to go.

Tenacity

One way to show immediate GRIT is to own, take charge of, and shape what you do with your autonomy, rather than letting it shape you. You define and lead your climb, your ascent. Start now by applying the tools in this chapter to start strong and finish even stronger.

Have a Sense of Personal Responsibility

Exhibit 1.1 illustrates some of the differences and similarities among high school, a full-time job, and college. As you take a look at the column labeled "college" in Exhibit 1.1, you'll notice that a pattern emerges—compared to their high school classes or full-time jobs, college students experience a dramatic increase in the amount of personal responsibility they must handle. High school teachers and job supervisors provide clear guidance, both about expectations and how to achieve them. In college, however, the student is responsible for understanding the expectations for academic and career success based on information from the college catalog, syllabi, and assignments and for developing a strategy for meeting those expectations.

There have probably been some times during your high school or work experience when you wished that you had more freedom to make your own decisions and pursue your own interests. As you step into college, these wishes indeed come true. The range of opportunities and alternatives that lie before you is so broad and diverse that you'll find yourself making important decisions every day.

This broad range of personal responsibility is exciting, but it can also become overwhelming at times, and you can find yourself suffering significant consequences for poor decisions along the way. It's important, then, to develop a personal approach that you can use as you step into an experience that offers so much personal responsibility and autonomy.

Complete the Meeting Expectations activity by choosing a college expectation that you will encounter and writing an action statement for how you will meet that expectation through personal responsibility.

EXHIBIT 1.1 Differences among High School, Full-Time Work, and College

High School	Full-Time Work	College
Attendance is mandatory to meet requirements.	Attendance is mandatory to stay employed.	Attendance may not be mandatory to meet requirements.
At least six continuous hours are spent in class each day.	At least eight continuous hours are spent at work each day.	Different amounts of time are spent in class and between classes each day.
Moderate to no outside work is necessary to complete requirements.	Moderate to no overtime work is necessary to complete job duties.	Substantial amount of outside work is necessary to complete assignments and be successful.
Teachers go over material and expect students to remember facts and information.	Employers provide basic information and expect employees to use it to complete their jobs effectively.	Professors provide concepts and theories and expect students to evaluate ideas, synthesize the ideas with other concepts they have learned, and develop new ideas.

Meeting
expectations

The college will expect that I . . .	To meet that expectation, I will . . .
Example: . . . read the assigned material before I get to class.	*Example:* . . . schedule time before every class to complete the required readings and review my notes.

Connect with Others

Even the most dedicated student cannot do it all alone. Climbers are typically "on rope" with others. In fact, behind every successful college graduate is a good support system, usually comprising family, friends, and community members. It is no secret that succeeding in college will take more than just studying hard—you will need to surround yourself with people who encourage you to do your best. There will be times when you need others for academic, emotional, and even financial support. Recognizing who in your circle of friends, family, and contacts will be the best resources for you is part of the process of creating a support system that will inevitably be part of your college success. Who will not just support but stretch you to do and become more?

PROFESSORS. There may be no one more important to your college and possible future career success than a professor. She does not just provide you with access to the content and challenge you to think critically about the subject matter, she also can be a mentor and a resource as you complete your degree and start your career. One way to start out on the right path to a good relationship is to greet your professor with a smile and a "hello" when you see her in and out of class.

ADVISORS, COUNSELORS, AND STAFF. In addition to professors, some of the most important relationships that you will forge during college will be with people whose sole job is to help you succeed. Counselors and advisors will be key people in your academic career, so be sure to take the time to get to know these individuals. College administrators also play an important role.

Your advisor may be the first person you encounter at college. An advisor explains to you what courses you should take, how many hours you should take a semester, and how to plan remaining semesters. You may be lucky enough to have the same advisor throughout your college career, in which case, regular contact with your advisor will help keep the lines of communication open. If you have a different advisor each semester, you may wish to find one person who can act as a regular advisor.

YOUR FAMILY. Whether you live with your parents, you are a parent, or you are somewhere in between, your family is an important part of who you are and what you will become. Your family has influenced your values and beliefs, and your family members may be a part of the reason you have enrolled in college. For many students, their ability to stay in college and be successful depends on the support of their family. If your family will be an important part of your life as you pursue a degree, then you will need to consider how they will support you and what you need to communicate with them about what to expect when you have to spend more time studying and taking classes than strengthening relationships with them.

the unwritten rules
of Motivation, Goals, and Mission Statements

- **Internal motivation is the key to success.** If most of your reasons for attending college are based on what others have told you, or if your motivations for succeeding in college are driven mostly by the expectations of others, you will need to dig deeper to discover the reasons why *you* want to succeed. This is where your GRIT and goals work together. Find your internal motivation for college success, even if it takes a while to discover it.

- **Goals are dreams with a deadline.** Setting goals to achieve your dream is the only way to make it happen. A student who says she wants to be a doctor will also need to describe when and how that will happen to ensure she has the best trail map to get to her destination.

- **Those who have mission statements will get where they want to go.** Your college has one, and most every business you patronize has one as well. Mission statements keep companies and institutions on track to meeting their goals. Having a personal mission statement will help you do the same and will help you determine what paths to take and decisions to make in the future.

YOUR FRIENDS. Another important part of your support system is your friends. Although you may not be able to choose your family members, you will have more choice as to which friends will be positive influences on your college experience. If you have friends who have also attended or are attending college, you will have a great opportunity to connect with each other on this common pursuit. Even if you do not attend the same college, you can develop a support system with them since you will all be having similar experiences. You can share advice and study strategies as well as have a shoulder to lean on when you feel stressed. Knowing that a friend is having a similar experience can often give you the motivation to continue working hard.

YOUR ROOMMATES. If you've chosen to live in a dorm or apartment during your college career, you'll discover that your roommates can be either very helpful or, unfortunately, very destructive influences on your life. Roommates who share the same goals and values as you and who are equally committed to being successful in college as you are can provide a strong support system for you. They can offer encouragement when you're feeling discouraged or companionship when you're feeling lonely. You can provide the same support to them. It will be important for you to have study habits and a personal strategy of your own, but at times you'll benefit greatly from sharing the college experience with your roommates, with whom you may share meals, social activities, and household chores.

GRIT GAINER™

CHOOSE YOUR ROPE TEAM When climbers get "on rope" with other people, they do two powerful things. First, they help each other climb. Second, when you slip, they immediately slow or stop the fall. You get to decide who is part of your ascent.

1. Who do you want "on rope" with you? Who elevates, challenges, supports, and believes in you?

2. Whom can you count on? Who will inspire you to climb further and higher than you might reach by yourself?

Your Personal Values and Motivation Can Help You Achieve Academic Success

Your Dreams Are Worth Pursuing

As you consider your goals, you will also want to think about your dreams. Dreams are the big ideas and bold achievements that you sometimes imagine and for which you secretly hope. What do you want to do or achieve that you have not written down because you feel it is too far-fetched? There are many stories of people who ignored their dreams and took jobs that provided them with financial security and prestige, only to discover that their lives were not fulfilled because they regretted giving up on their dreams. There are also many exciting stories about people who never forgot their dreams and who eventually achieved them through hard work and determination.

Why don't more people follow their dreams? First, they may not know what their dreams are. Sometimes day-to-day life takes up so much of their time, attention, and energy that they don't take time to consider their dreams. Second, these same people may be scared. Pursuing your dreams is a risky proposition, and there's always the chance that circumstances or events could bring disappointment and failure in this pursuit. Third, some people need to make the "safe" choice first before they feel confident that they can pursue their dreams. Although you may not be able to fulfill your dreams in the immediate future, don't lose sight of them.

© ERASHOV/SHUTTERSTOCK

■ The only way to know if you are successful is to have a goal to aim for.

Your Values Drive Your Goals

Part of your life story will include your value system. Values can be inherited from your parents, or they can come from what your culture, religion, or ethnicity regard as important. Values can also be formed from both positive and negative experiences. For example, you may value honesty, which means that you try to be truthful and straightforward in most situations

integrity matters

Staying true to your values is part of having integrity. If you try to please others or adopt their values without completely agreeing with them, you will lack integrity. For example, you may have been raised with the value of staying true to your identity, even at the expense of not being accepted by a group you aspire to. Now that you are in college, you may find that you are exposed to a variety of people with different perspectives and experiences and that you enjoy and appreciate learning more about others and those experiences.

YOUR TURN

In approximately 250 words, discuss a time in which you took on someone else's values. Discuss your motivations for doing so, as well as the outcome. Finally, explain what you learned in the process.

GRIT GAINER™

IMAGINE YOUR MOUNTAIN You want who you are and what you do to make some sort of difference. Your highest aspiration defines your mountain. You want to move forward and up in life, to ascend. Staying true to your values, dreams, and purpose is difficult. The weather on the mountain can be harsh. Some people quit. Most go partway and camp; they stop short and play it safe. Be a *climber*. It takes some serious GRIT. But the views are unmatched.

Resilience

and that you expect others to be honest with you. If you value hard work, then you strive to do your best in your life. If a friend has treated you with compassion, you may value sensitivity to others. On the other hand, if you have been discriminated against in the past, you may now value open-mindedness in others.

Whatever values you claim can be pretty meaningless until tested by adversity. It is in these moments of truth that you and the people in your life get to see who you really are and what you truly stand for. Be ready to sacrifice for what you believe in. This makes your values real.

The importance of knowing and understanding your values is that this knowledge can help you set realistic goals. If you value a satisfying career, for instance, you will set goals that support that value. Therefore, you will probably investigate careers and fields that are challenging and interesting. If you value a stable financial future, you will set goals that enable you to earn enough money to provide for your needs and wants. If you value your family, you will make spending time with them a priority. Your values should be a true reflection of who *you* are and what *you* believe.

Your Motivation Fuels Action

Motivation is the driving force behind action. You will not act unless you are motivated to do so. Your motivation determines whether you will put forth the thought, time, and effort to achieve your goals and dreams. When was the last time you felt really motivated to do something? Maybe you just watched an inspirational movie, received a raise at work, or you received some encouraging words from a friend or relative. Or perhaps an event or circumstance—like running into an old friend whose life has turned in a bad direction—helped you realize that you need to take action to avoid similar circumstances in your life. Regardless of the source of your motivation, you are more compelled to take action in pursuit of your dreams when you feel motivated.

Resilience

Of course, no matter how gritty you may be, there may be times in your academic career when you feel overwhelmed by your responsibilities and unsure of your ability to handle it all. That's normal. When you feel weighed down by all that you have to accomplish for a particular week or day, try to calm down first. If you can, talk with a friend, an instructor, or a counselor and explain your frustration and stress. To stay motivated and to resist the temptation to give up, remind yourself of why you are doing what you are doing.

When things pile up, ask yourself these gritty, resilience-building questions:

1. What are the facets of the situation I can potentially influence?
2. Where and how can I step up to get some immediate traction?
3. How can I get past this as quickly as possible?

It might be helpful to revisit Activity 1.1 that you completed earlier in the chapter. Your answers to the fourth or fifth level of "why" may provide clues to help you uncover the real reasons why you are in college, why you want to succeed, and what you want to accomplish.

the unwritten rules
of Motivation, Goals, and Mission Statements

- **Everyone is motivated by something.** Goals are dreams with a deadline: Your professors have their own motivations and goals that can help you understand them better, but they may not tell you what they are or have them written down. As you get to know your professors in class, during office hours, or in their role as faculty advisors to student clubs and organizations, ask questions and listen for clues to help you understand what motivates your professors. Setting goals to achieve your dream is the only way to make it happen. A student who says she wants to be a doctor will also need to describe when and how that will happen to ensure she has the best road map to get to her destination.

- **Relationships and motivation go hand in hand.** Those who have mission statements will get where they want to go: If you can uncover and understand what motivates someone and what that person is trying to accomplish in her life, you will be better equipped to have a good personal and working relationship with that person. A great way to have good relationships with all of these people is to understand them and to know what drives them. Your college has one and most every business you patronize has one as well. Mission statements keep companies and institutions on track to meeting their goals. Having a personal mission statement will help you do the same and will help you determine what paths to take and decisions to make in the future.

Set "SMART" Gritty Goals for Your Success

Your Goals Set the Bar for Achievement

To build on your mission statement—and to fulfill that mission in the process—you will need to set goals that elevate you, goals you want to strive for and achieve. They need to be tough enough to stretch you, help you grow, and bring out your best.

A goal is something that you work toward—it may be to learn how to cook macaroni and cheese, to quit a bad habit, or to write a novel. Whatever your goals, they should be reasonable and attainable in the time frame that you have assigned. For instance, if you want to lose 10 pounds in one week, you may need to rethink the time in which you would like to achieve your goal. A more reasonable goal would be to lose 10 pounds in four months. Reasonable goals are more likely to be met.

As you begin to think about your goals, consider dividing them into long-term goals and short-term goals. Certainly, one of your long-term goals is to earn a degree. This goal may take one year or more, depending on how many degree requirements you need to complete or how many other responsibilities you may have.

When you make a list of your goals, follow the "SMART" acronym. Your goals should be specific, measurable, attainable, realistic, and time-specific:

Specific: A goal should describe one specific outcome, such as losing 12 pounds.

Measurable: A goal should describe an outcome that is observable and measurable. For example, weight loss can be measured on a scale.

Attainable: A goal can be challenging, but also something that you believe you can achieve. Losing weight—no matter how little—is attainable for most people.

Growth

Realistic: Losing 12 pounds in two weeks is probably unrealistic and even unhealthy, but losing 12 pounds within 12 weeks is more likely to be realistic.

Time-specific: A goal should specify the time frame for achievement, so that you can gauge your progress and success. If your goal is simply to lose 12 pounds, but you don't specify a time period, you won't know whether you're on track to achieve it or what your deadline is for achieving it. Establish a measurable deadline so you can celebrate your accomplishment on that day or time!

Below are three goals that a college student might set for him- or herself. Let's apply the SMART approach to improve each one:

- "Get good grades in college." This is a noble goal, certainly, but it's neither measurable nor time-specific. "Achieve a 3.4 GPA at the end of my first term" would specify how you'll measure the goal (GPA) and by when (at the end of your first term).

- "Earn extra money to pay for college." A lot of students will have this kind of goal for their college experience, but the goal needs to be measurable and time-specific. "Generate an extra $2,000 in income before the beginning of fall semester" would establish a specific measure and a timeline.

- "Build a network of people who can help me get a job." Business students in particular are often told about the importance of "networking," but it can be a challenge to express that activity as a goal. It might be helpful to break the activity into some specific action items and use them to establish goals. For example, a first-year student could get her networking success on track by setting the following goal: "Personally meet and obtain business cards from at least 10 business or community leaders by the end of this academic year."

My GOALS

© VICHIE81/SHUTTERSTOCK

Write down specific, measurable goals and mark them off as you meet them.

Here are a few other tips for writing effective goals:

- **Write your goals down.** No matter what you want to achieve, be sure that you write down all your goals and review them every few months to assess your progress.

- **Break larger goals into smaller goals that will lead to fulfillment.** Smaller goals are easier to achieve and they can build quickly into a larger, long-term goal.

- **Regularly review your goals and make changes as necessary.** Circumstances will occur beyond your control that will require you to adjust your plans. A big part of GRIT is adjusting your path as things change but remaining relentless in completing your goals. You may set goals now that change over time as you discover new things about yourself or learn about new career and personal opportunities.

- **Reach out to others who care about you to help you achieve your goals.** Communicate your goals to your coworkers, family, and friends. Enlist them to help you meet your goals, especially if you need to schedule time to study and complete assignments. Managing your time will be much easier if your priorities and goals are concrete, realistic, and communicated to those around you.

Growth

- **Identify habits or challenges that could interfere with your goals.** As you work toward your goals, make an effort to eliminate anything that keeps you from focusing on your goals. If you think you don't have time to accomplish two short-term goals during the week, examine where you have been spending your time and eliminate the activities that do not contribute to your goals. If you watch seven hours of television a week, and you aren't achieving the sought-after short-term goal of becoming more informed, then spend that time doing something that does contribute to your goals.

Complete Activity 1.2 by identifying three goals you would like to meet this term. Be sure to follow the SMART goal guidelines.

Write a Personal Mission Statement

Your Mission Statement Defines Your Purpose

Mission statements are statements of purpose. Most companies develop a mission statement for themselves because it defines their purpose and answers the crucial questions: "Why do I exist?" and "What is my purpose?" Your personal mission statement should explain your purpose in life from a very broad perspective. Your mission statement describes how your values and goals will create your life's mission. Once you've identified your values, your motivations, and your goals, your next step is to describe your mission statement to establish your purpose.

It's in the syllabus

Your professors' syllabi provide a number of clues that can help you develop SMART goals for academic success. For example, a syllabus for biology might list due dates and requirements for assignments, projects, or exams. You could establish some SMART goals that would help you succeed in that class, such as "Review a draft of my DNA project with my professor at least one week before it is due."

- What are the most important graded activities in your class?
- When are they due? What specific goals can you work toward to help you earn high scores on those graded activities?

EXHIBIT 1.2 SMART Goal and Action Plan

LONG-TERM SMART GOAL: Graduate with a bachelor's degree in biology by May 2018	
Action Steps	
Register by April 2015 for summer 2015 classes to get ahead on my degree plan	Meet with my advisor June 2015 to plan my schedule for fall 2015 and spring 2016
Register for required courses for fall 2016 by April 2016	Register by April 2016 for summer 2016 classes to get ahead on my degree plan or to retake any classes I need to retake
Meet with an advisor May 2017 to ensure I am on track to graduate in May 2018	Apply for graduation by February 2018

■ ACTIVITY 1.2 Three SMART Goals for the Semester

Goals
SMART Goal 1
SMART Goal 2
SMART Goal 3

As you meet your goals and learn new things, your mission will likely change and your mission statement will need to be revised. The following is an example of a mission statement that you can use as a model for defining your own mountain.

Sample Life's Mission Statement
As nurse and educator, my life's mission is to work in a large research hospital and teach future nurses. By supporting my values of caring for others, education, and job security, I work toward my life's mission by completing my nursing degree, working in different hospital environments, and training other nurses.

Practice writing your own mission statement in Activity 1.3 by filling in the blanks with the information that is suggested. Use your work below to revise and refine your mission statement as you begin to meet your goals.

■ **ACTIVITY 1.3   My Mission Statement**

My Mission Statement

As a _____(dream/career/job/role), my life's

mission is to _____ (long-term goal). By supporting

my values of _____, _____, and _____,

I work toward my life's mission by _____, _____,

and _____ (short-term goals).

Because your mission statement describes your purpose in life, it's a personalized statement that captures your own dreams, values, and goals. Your mission statement serves as a trail map that you can review on a regular basis to help you evaluate your life and whether the activities and efforts you are investing in on a daily basis are contributing to your purpose in life, or if they are actually hindering your pursuit of your purpose. Take some time to write your personal mission statement and share it with some people in your life who are trustworthy and supportive of your success. Invite their input, make changes as needed, and then keep the final version somewhere that you can access regularly to remind yourself of your purpose in life.

GRIT GAINER™

GRIT YOUR GOALS   GRIT is the most important factor in completing your goals and fulfilling your dreams. Try these two tips to put some GRIT in your goals. Before you decide on or finalize your goals, ask yourself:

1. How can I kick it up a notch and stretch myself by making this goal a little more challenging?

2. If my life depended on me getting this goal accomplished quickly (and well), how much sooner could I get it done?

You'll be amazed at how your capacity to climb continues to grow.

THE GRIT ADVANTAGE

You want to move forward and up in life, and college will help you get there. You can decide now: how far and high do you want to climb? Don't quit. Don't camp. Do what climbers do:

- *Define your mountain.* Don't let your past define your future. How do you want your life? What do you want it to be all about?

- *Establish your trail map.* Lay out your strategy, set specific, measurable mileposts along the way, and stretch yourself to accomplish more, more quickly than you imagined.

- *Build your rope team.* Decide whom you trust, respect, and want to join up with to help you achieve or surpass your goals.

- *Assess yourself.* Find out your learning preference by completing the personal inventory. Then go beyond the labels. Take on the uncomfortable. Stretch your capacities so you can climb strong.

HOW GRITTY ARE YOU?

It's time to climb! Now that you've completed this chapter, how committed are you to:

1. Defining your mountain by beginning to shape your personal mission statement?

   Zero Commitment 0 ———————————————————————————— 10 Fully Committed

2. Reassessing and rerouting when needed to stay true to your goals?

   Zero Commitment 0 ———————————————————————————— 10 Fully Committed

3. Spending time and energy climbing, rather than camping or quitting?

   Zero Commitment 0 ———————————————————————————— 10 Fully Committed

4. Showing moral fortitude, but living your values in the moments of truth?

   Zero Commitment 0 ———————————————————————————— 10 Fully Committed

5. Taking advantage of the support system and resources around you?

   Zero Commitment 0 ———————————————————————————— 10 Fully Committed

6. Picking a strong "rope team," people you can join up with to do great things, and who support your goals?

   Zero Commitment 0 ———————————————————————————— 10 Fully Committed

7. Understanding, using, and expanding your intelligences, capabilities, learning preferences, and more?

   Zero Commitment 0 ———————————————————————————— 10 Fully Committed

2 Time Management

Chapter goals to help you get in, get through, get out, and get paid:

This chapter will help you become an effective time manager so you can get in, get through, get out, and get paid. To graduate, you need to complete all of the courses in your degree plan, and each of these courses will require you to keep track of and meet deadlines for assignments, exams, and other activities.

To get a great job, you'll need to manage your time well so that you can simultaneously complete your degree requirements and engage in a successful job search. And once you land the job you're looking for, you'll need to be an effective time manager to meet the expectations that your manager and coworkers will have for you.

To meet those goals, this chapter will help you:

- Recognize the importance of effective time management for college success
- Set priorities
- Make use of tools and routines to manage your time effectively
- Avoid time management pitfalls
- Exercise "**smart GRIT**" to put your time and energy to optimal use

MyStudentSuccessLab™

Log in to MyStudentSuccessLab.com to deepen your **GRIT** mindset and build the skills you'll need to get through the college experience.

Laura's Story

Pouring her fourth cup of coffee at 11:00 P.M., Laura searches for her history paper assignment. It's due at 9:00 A.M. tomorrow. She sinks into her chair to go through her backpack one more time and debates whether to call a classmate for help.

Laura doesn't normally procrastinate on her school work, but her middle child has been sick for two days and she's been home caring for him.

Three hours later, Laura's paper is finished. As she prints her final copy, the printer begins to screech loudly and stops. Frantic, she rips the page from the printer. When she presses "print" again, the first three words barely appear on the page before the ink completely disappears.

The only thing she can do is to save her paper to a thumb drive and hope that tomorrow provides her with a solution.

Before her head reaches the pillow, she remembers a flyer she found for the campus computer lab, which opens at 7:00 A.M. Because she gets to campus early, she is able to print off the remaining page in the computer lab—thanks to some help from the lab assistant.

"I will return your papers next week," says her professor. "In the meantime, you may want to get started on your next paper assignment on Greek culture."

Now, what do you think?

- What would you do if you faced a technical glitch right before an important assignment was due?
  a. Explain to my professor why I couldn't get it in on time and plead for more time
  b. Come up with a Plan A and Plan B for first thing in the morning to make sure I get my assignment in no matter what
  c. Pull out my schedule and make some tweaks to make sure I don't end up in the same spot on my other assignments
  d. Reach out to a fellow (good) student to either 1) help me get it printed so I can sleep better, or 2) work together on future assignments so we can help each other through any challenges

- If you wanted to be sure that you are not in the same predicament again, what would you do?
  a. Do the same thing as I did before, because this was a one-time event
  b. Make sure that next time I don't create unnecessary stress by waiting until the last minute
  c. Start working earlier on my assignments so that personal and technical challenges do not make me stumble
  d. Work on assignments with a classmate so that we can rely on each other if we run into challenges

Now Is the Time to Develop an Effective Time Management Strategy

When asked, the number one issue and biggest challenge college students say they face is *time management*. Why?

- **The college experience adds new and different responsibilities to an already busy life.** Even before you stepped onto campus, you probably felt like your life was busy. Now you are a full-time college student on top of a full-time life.

- **The college experience brings high expectations.** Whatever your past level of motivation, college will likely require more. Even if you are a highly motivated, success-oriented person, you're already placing high expectations on yourself. Now, in addition to your own expectations, your professors, advisors, parents, and other people who care about you will also place their expectations on you to succeed.

- **The college experience includes a wide variety of responsibilities.** As a full-time student, you're taking three to five different classes—each with its own requirements and schedules—and you may be involved in clubs or other student organizations, working, and juggling family and social responsibilities as well.

- **The college experience puts you in charge.** You have far more autonomy to make decisions about how you spend your time in a college setting than you did previously

Meeting expectations

The college will expect that I . . .	To meet that expectation, I will . . .
Example: . . . turn in assignments on time.	*Example:* . . . post assignments on my calendar system as soon as I get them and schedule blocks of time well before the due date to start working on them.
_____	_____
_____	_____
_____	_____

Tenacity

To face the time management challenge, you need to not only develop the skillset, you need to develop a gritty mindset, growing the discipline and tenacity to get the important things done, and done right.

It's in the syllabus

Look at the syllabus for each of your courses to help determine what your priorities and tasks will be each week. Record the deadlines from every class in a single calendar system. Chances are, there will be certain weeks when deadlines overlap, and you'll find yourself needing to take an exam and finish a project in the same week. By planning ahead, you can work on some of these assignments ahead of time to protect yourself from having to complete several important activities at once.

- How much time do you anticipate spending on each course?
- What days or weeks will be particularly busy for you?
- What additional obligations will you have during those busy times?
- How will you manage your priorities and time?

in high school or work. This freedom can be exciting, but it also brings a new level of responsibility for managing your time without direct supervision from either your parents or an employer.

- **The college experience is academically demanding.** A lot of assignments are bigger, tougher, more complicated, may require a lot of group work, and take longer than what you may have been required to do up until now.

This chapter will help you with both your time management skillset and mindset.

An effective time management strategy will help you become productive (get a lot done), effective (do it well), and satisfied (feel good about it) in your personal and academic life. One of the main reasons that an effective time management strategy helps you feel satisfied is because it helps you feel in control. Growing your GRIT will help you both respond well when things go wrong and stay on track, no matter what.

Your time management strategy is your plan for using your most valuable resource—your time—to fulfill your personal mission statement and to achieve your goals (SMART goals, of course!). How you use and organize your time will depend on your goals—such a completing your degree, securing a job, and building relationships—and your personal mission statement, which defines your purpose and values in your life. For example, if your personal mission statement places a high degree of importance on helping others and giving back to society, your allocation of time to activities that reflect those values should be consistent.

Throughout this chapter, be sure to keep your goals and mission statement in sight, as they should serve as the compass to guide your time management decisions.

Know Your Priorities

You may already have some kind of system for keeping track of all the various tasks you have to complete, activities you need to attend, or people you need to contact. All of these items typically end up on your to-do list, or on a scattered selection of Post-it notes located around your dorm or car interior. You already know from experience that not every task or responsibility on your list is of equal importance. To be successful in school and in life, you need to keep your focus on the most important—and not necessarily the most urgent—responsibilities and activities in your life.

Some responsibilities might be urgent but not important, whereas others may be important but not urgent. An urgent responsibility tries to demand your time and energy right now. Your friends may be texting you to make plans for the evening, and they want you to reply right away. But you may be devoting your attention at the moment to developing long-term goals and a personal mission statement. What should you do—reply to the text message or keep working on your goals and mission statement? This is a clear decision between the urgent and the important, and you make hundreds of these types of decisions every day. The more you keep your focus on achieving what's important and keeping the urgent within a manageable limit, the more success you will experience.

© ALEX HINDS/SHUTTERSTOCK

Your college activities will keep you busy, so it will be best to create a system to help you juggle it all.

The distinction between the urgent and the important will help you engage in an important activity—prioritizing. A priority is something that is important and urgent at that moment. Prioritizing is the activity of ranking or sorting responsibilities and activities from the greatest to the least importance to help you decide what to do, when, and what to work on first. As you step into the college experience, the number of activities and responsibilities competing for your time and attention will quickly multiply. Your ability to prioritize will be critically important to helping you succeed. You will need to continually review the list of activities and responsibilities in your life and keep them ranked and sorted according to their importance.

Here's an example of a prioritization strategy you may want to try. Select a syllabus from one of the classes you're taking this semester and find the "grading" section. Professors typically provide information about how they will determine grades in the class, including the relative contribution of individual assignments, quizzes, exams, and projects to your total grade. For example, the final exam in your calculus course might account for 25 percent of your grade, compared to one of the quizzes that is worth 3 percent. Which of these two is most important? Clearly, because the final exam contributes to a far greater proportion of your grade than an individual quiz, the exam is more important. This technique of comparing individual assignments, projects, and exams on the basis of their point value or contribution to your total grade is one example of a technique that can help you prioritize your work.

integrity matters

If you tend to use your smartphone or other electronic devices while you're talking to someone in person at the same time, you should know that this type of behavior may be considered rude and disrespectful, even an issue of personal integrity, by professors and college staff. Why? You are signaling to that person that they are not important enough to warrant your full attention. One way to maintain integrity—and be respectful—is to turn your cell phone off and put it in your backpack when you visit with your professor during office hours and when you attend class.

YOUR TURN

In approximately 250 words, describe how you feel when others have not given you their undivided attention when you have wanted it.

Growth

It is your mindset that will determine how well you put your skillset—these tools and tactics—to use. GRIT applies to everything you care about in life. But it is particularly important to time (and life) management.

Deadlines, of course, are another important consideration for prioritizing. In general, assignments or responsibilities that have a more immediate deadline should be a higher priority than responsibilities that are due later. However, this is the time when you need to differentiate between the urgent and the important. If you only focus on those responsibilities that have near-term deadlines, you won't have much time to work on activities that are more important, such as setting long-term goals and conducting research to help you plan your career. One approach to this challenge is to give yourself a fixed amount of time each day to tackle the urgent issues in your life while also scheduling time for important but not urgent activities.

Tools Can Help You Manage Time

As you implement your time management strategy, you can draw on the help of a wide variety of tools to help you achieve your goals. The best time managers and students relentlessly plan and spend their time on the right things: those that are most critical to fulfilling their main goals. They refuse to be pulled off course by the countless distractions and time wasters that spring up in the course of a normal week. Tools can show you how to make stuff fit. But your success depends on bringing a decent dose of GRIT.

Calendars, Lists, and Work Space

If you use a paper calendar, you have many different types from which to choose. Once you determine the type that works best for you—a monthly, weekly, or daily calendar—make a habit of writing down your tasks, no matter how big or small. Here is an example of a typical list of a day's activities for a student like Laura:

Thursday

- Make appointment to have oil changed
- Pick up medicine for Mom
- Turn in housing deposit for next semester
- Study for history quiz on Friday
- Write essay for English Composition
- Turn in student club membership application

A typical monthly calendar allows you to see several weeks at once so that you can remain aware of upcoming events, but often there is little space on a monthly calendar to write down detailed lists such as the one above.

A weekly calendar allows you to glance at one week at a time. A benefit to a weekly calendar is that you can have room to write out details of each activity; however, a drawback to a weekly calendar is it is difficult to anticipate what you must do the next week.

Daily calendars usually provide the most space to write your day-to-day tasks and appointments. This kind of calendar may be the most difficult to work with if you need to plan ahead. Because you cannot see the rest of the week or month, you may overlook important events or be surprised by them. Use a daily calendar if you are extremely organized and can plan ahead effectively, or use it in addition to a monthly calendar.

If you have reliable Internet access in your home, apartment, or dorm and access to computers while on campus in computer labs, you may want to consider using a web-based electronic calendar system and priority list; also, consider using your phone's calendar to help you stay on track. In many cases, those phone calendars can sync to your computer, which will allow you to stay updated no matter what device you use. These calendars allow you to quickly toggle between views of your day, week, and month, and can separate your school demands and personal life. Electronic calendars allow you to set up events to automatically repeat themselves (e.g., calculus quiz every Thursday; Dad's birthday on March 18), rearrange priority lists without having to rewrite them, set up reminders and alerts to prompt you about upcoming deadlines and events, and share your calendar with others so that you can coordinate team projects and family responsibilities. The added benefit of a web-based system is that you can access it anytime and anywhere you have Internet access.

Once you've chosen a calendar system that works best for you, find your university's academic calendar on the campus website or in the catalog and add the following deadlines to your schedule:

Completed	Important Dates Checklist
✓	Deadlines for registering and filing financial aid forms
✓	Date for the beginning of classes (or instruction)
✓	Drop/add dates for changing your schedule
✓	Due dates for tuition payment
✓	Withdrawal dates for leaving college before the semester is over
✓	Registration dates for the next semester
✓	School holidays or breaks

There is no doubt that the most effective people—those who get the most done in the least amount of time—make constant and immediate use of their own calendars. They persistently plan. They use their calendars to be more resilient, adjusting plans to stay on track as factors change. Every time anything pops up (a new appointment, a changed date, a test or assignment) whip out and add it to your calendar, now! Life is fluid. And it feels great to stay on top as things unfold.

The ideal calendar and priority list are first steps to managing your time well, but there is more you can do. Creating a quiet, clutter-free space where you can study and complete assignments will also help you manage your time effectively and efficiently. If you don't have a place in your house or apartment that you can call your own and a comfortable chair or seat at the kitchen table is all that you can spare, make sure it is comfortable and quiet and has adequate space for books, notebooks, and other supplies. It has to be a place where you want to be or it will be difficult to go there to stay on task.

Instinct

The reality is, you may not always have an ideal learning or work space to accomplish your tasks. Things and people unexpectedly intrude. Sometimes you have to either agilely adjust the situation (like go somewhere else, rather than just suffer) or dig deep and do whatever it takes to achieve your goal.

Routines Are Also Time Management Tools

With an effective calendar and priority list in place, you can now start to establish a time management routine that helps you stay on track and maintain control over your life. For your calendar and task list to be effective, you need to establish a daily routine of reviewing and updating this information. Take a few minutes every evening to review what you've accomplished and check those items off your priority list (this will be a very satisfying experience!), add new tasks that came up that day, and then review tomorrow's calendar and priority list so you can anticipate tomorrow's goals.

Knowing what to expect for the day will make surprises less likely. Also, if you know that you have an early start tomorrow, you can make special preparations, such as preparing a lunch the night before, getting your backpack organized, making sure you know where you have to go by reviewing a map, and setting your alarm (and backups, if you tend to hit the snooze button a lot!). Stressful mornings tend to get you on the wrong track for the day, and they can typically be avoided with some thoughtful planning the night before.

The second element of your time management routine that can help you manage your stress, keep you resilient, and put you in control of your schedule is a strategy called *back planning*. The basic premise of back planning is to look ahead at a deadline for a task, estimate the amount of time it will take to complete the task, and establish a starting point for the task. For example, if you know that you need to write a 20-page paper for English composition, and you expect that all of the research, writing, editing, formatting, and printing will take two weeks, you can schedule time to start the project at least two weeks before its deadline.

Back planning also works for short-term planning—if you know that your morning class starts at 8:30, and it typically takes 45 minutes for you to complete your entire morning routine and find parking, then you know that you need to be walking out the door of your dorm or apartment no later than 7:45 to be on time for class. Establishing these milestones will help you stay on track to meet deadlines and reduce the stress that's often associated with running behind in your schedule.

Resilience

Expect the unexpected. Don't be thrown off if you are forced to change your plan. Gritty students know and mentally prepare for the unexpected. When something threatens to throw you off, ask yourself, "How can I get back on track as quickly as possible?" Then adjust your schedule accordingly.

the unwritten rules
about Time Management

- **Projects, midterms, and finals will all tend to collide at the same time each term.** The best way to not only survive but succeed each term is to start early on your projects and assignments and review your notes and class materials each week so that studying for midterms and finals will not require as much time or effort.

- **The best opportunities for accomplishing the important items on your priority list may occur between terms.** Look for opportunities during spring break, holiday breaks, summer, and even three-day weekends to get some solitude and quiet and to revisit the important-but-not-urgent items on your list, like your personal mission statement, SMART goals, and career plan.

- **No matter how well you think you can work under pressure, professors can detect procrastination from a mile away.** You'll be at a disadvantage as soon as the professor sees the evidence of procrastination. Most importantly, if you wait too long to start or complete an assignment, you forego the biggest advantage of getting an early start—the opportunity to get helpful feedback from your professor on preliminary drafts of your work. Melinda Beck (2012) states that "[t]oo much stress, fatigue, and time pressure can kill creativity: A little bit of stress might help to get you motivated, but too much of it will typically cause you to shut down."

- **Even with today's technology, it takes time to learn.** In his comprehensive study of student success chronicled in the book *What Matters in College*, Alexander Astin (1997) found that the amount of time students spend practicing what they are trying to learn, or "time on task," is the single greatest predictor of academic success. It takes a lot of GRIT to succeed. You have to dig deep and stick with it. Sorry, no shortcuts here.

Looking Out for Time Management Pitfalls

Avoid the "Black Holes" of Technology and Procrastination

Often portrayed in science fiction movies or scientific documentaries, black holes in space absorb everything around them, including light. From the perspective of time and energy management, television, videogames, and social media have the potential to be virtual black holes in your life that can consume far too much of your time and energy. If you plan on watching TV or connecting with friends online for only 10 minutes, it's really easy to discover that you're still sitting in front of the screen two hours later, and you've accomplished nothing during that time.

Videogames have the capacity to be even more time consuming because of their interactive nature. Social media like Facebook and Twitter have emerged as another potential black hole, consuming both your time and attention by feeding continual distractions to you throughout the day. As you establish your time and energy management strategies for the college experience, we urge extreme caution in your use of any of these three items. They are popular activities among college students, certainly, but if they aren't consumed in careful moderation, they can absorb your time and energy and leave you with little in return for your academic pursuits.

Instinct

You can let your distractions own you, or you can own them. Let "screen time" (or whatever your vice) be your reward at the end of a gritty, productive day. Save your lowest energy hours for those activities, and your prime energy hours for those things that create real momentum toward your goals.

Media and technology are not the only ways to avoid doing your work in college; in fact, you will most likely find a variety of ways to procrastinate. Activities such as cramming for quizzes and exams, pulling all-nighters to finish a paper or project, and missing work or other classes to finish an assignment on the due date are all evidence of procrastination. These types of last-minute, hurried efforts to meet a deadline tend to yield relatively poor academic performance and generate a tremendous amount of emotional, physical, and social stress. However, these desperate strategies are avoidable! With effective back planning, you can alleviate the need to stay up all night before an exam or miss other classes to finish an assignment.

The single biggest obstacle you need to overcome to avoid procrastination is starting the project. Procrastination typically occurs when we (yes, professors sometimes procrastinate, too) are confused, intimidated, or overwhelmed by an assignment or task. Our fears get the best of us, and we choose to forget about the assignment for a while instead of trying to get started. Once we do get started on a project, the fears tend to dissipate, and we discover that we're making more progress than we expected. The problem with procrastination is that if we wait a long time before starting the project, the fear of missing the deadline and being late begins to creep in and we lose our ability to be creative problem solvers. That's not a very gritty approach. If you've ever tried to remember a phone number, locker combination, or some other mental note, you've probably discovered that it's more difficult to think clearly and solve problems when you're in a hurry or panicked. In the same way, it's difficult to be thoughtful and creative when you're trying to study for an exam or write a paper under excessive time pressure. The good news is, the grittier you become, the more you will flourish under pressure, and the less stressful it will feel.

Although it may seem like you can multitask and stay on track with your college work, you may find it more difficult to stay focused and complete tasks with so many distractions.

© MARCIO EUGENIO/SHUTTERSTOCK

GRIT GAINER™

BEAT THE CROWD There's an old saying, "The task expands to fill the time." So, you can shrink the time by shrinking the task. There are two kinds of GRIT: dumb GRIT and smart GRIT. Dumb GRIT is when you keep doing what everyone else does. Crowds are slow. Smart GRIT is when you do it quicker and better than almost everyone else.

1. Be the first in line for everything; 15 minutes early is better than 60 minutes in line.

2. Plan the ideal, quickest route between classes and other appointments. Get there faster and sooner; it can save you hours.

3. Get the resources (books, people, supplies, etc.), answers, and specific requirements for each assignment now, so you can save time later.

4. Plan persistently. Don't live by the question, "How long will this take?" The moment anything changes in your schedule, adjust and ask yourself, "Where, how, and when can I get this task done as efficiently and effectively as possible?"

We've spent a lot of time on procrastination, because it's such a common phenomenon in college, and we regularly see our students suffer significant and unnecessary consequences by putting things off. Show some GRIT. Refuse to fall into that abyss.

When you are assigned homework, projects, or papers, take time to use back planning and clearly establish your start date for the project, as well as important milestones along the way (e.g., first two chapters by September 15). Build those milestones into your calendar system, set time aside for the work, and dig in. If you can establish a solid routine of regularly reviewing your calendar and to-do list and using back planning, you'll be taking control of your time and developing skills that will serve you well in both college and throughout your life.

Multitasking Should Be Used in Moderation

The process of multitasking—simultaneously managing several tasks or devoting your attention to more than one activity at a time—is often lauded as an admirable and even necessary skill. In fact, many people believe that you can get more done and be more productive while multitasking; however, the scientific evidence doesn't support this premise. The brain cannot actually multitask. It switches between tasks. This means you have to turn off one thing to do the other thing. Research shows multitasking wastes time and produces inferior results.

If you have a tendency to check your emails, respond to text messages, monitor your Facebook status, and listen to music while attempting to write, study, or organize your calendar, you are undermining your ability to perform well because these simultaneous tasks are sapping both your time and energy. Take the time to shut down the peripheral activities and stimuli to focus on the primary task at hand and you'll find yourself accomplishing far more than you expected.

■ Getting and staying organized will help you manage your time well.

© MICHAL POPIEL/SHUTTERSTOCK

Manage Your Energy

Just as important as managing your time is managing, and ideally optimizing, your energy. Think about this scenario: You have all weekend off from work and your spouse has taken the kids to visit the grandparents. Therefore, you have 48 hours of complete solitude to write a research paper that is due on Monday. Sounds ideal, doesn't it? But what if you have the flu for those two days? Does the time mean anything when you don't have the energy to do the work? What if, instead of having the flu, you pulled two double shifts and haven't slept more than five hours in two days? Will you be able to use your free 48 hours productively working or will you need to pause to take care of yourself?

Time is only valuable if you have the energy to use it well. Energy includes both physical and mental stamina, strength, sharpness, and focus. Everyone experiences variations in how "sharp" he or she feels throughout the day. Researchers sometimes refer to this as our *circadian rhythm*. The key point is to understand yourself well enough to know when you are at the peak of your mental and physical alertness and when you're not.

In addition to the time of day, your energy levels rise and fall during the week. Do you find yourself tired on Monday mornings, but full of energy on Fridays? Or do you feel worn out by Thursday evenings, but rejuvenated on Sundays? Depending on your work, school, and personal schedules, you will find that you have regular bursts of energy at certain times of the week.

Growth

Once you've identified the hours in the day and the days in the week when you tend to be at your best, you can build your schedule to maximize your productivity during those times and schedule activities that don't require as much effort or concentration during times when you aren't at your peak. Activities such as writing papers, solving complex math problems, and reading articles and books for class assignments should be reserved for those peak times. It's during these times that you will also most need your quiet, uncluttered work space.

> It takes GRIT to find a way to do what you have to do when you're tired, your energy is low, and the last thing you want to do is school work. The gritty reality of school and life is sometimes it's messy and tough. But the best students are not usually the ones with the highest IQs. They are the ones who plan their time and energy intelligently, then refuse to make excuses when things don't go their way. They get it done.

Make that time sacred. This will require some discipline and advanced planning, because you'll be tempted by other tasks and distractions. Take advantage of your mental and physical sharpness during these peak periods to perform activities that will clearly help you get through, get out, and get paid. It will save you time. Most students are at or near the peak of their mental alertness shortly after waking up in the morning. If that's also the case for you, commit yourself to tackling the most important task of the day first thing in the morning. Consider signing up for early morning classes.

What should you do during those times when you aren't at your peak? First of all, recognize that it's OK to have some periods of time when you take a break from working hard. In fact, it's actually more productive to take breaks than to try to work hard all day. The good news is that you can still get a lot accomplished, even during times when you don't feel mentally or physically sharp. During those times, you can accommodate the common "time zappers" that can rob college students of their time: reviewing and sending emails, making phone calls, running errands, preparing meals, talking with roommates, taking a walk, swimming, or doing some other form of meditative exercise.

Growth

One way to help yourself manage your energy is by becoming aware of what activities relax you when you are stressed and what activities allow you to refill your energy reserves. If an activity rejuvenates you and helps you recharge, you may want to schedule the activity for times when you need more energy. If an activity helps you wind down, you may want to schedule it for after you have completed major tasks.

> Build the energy flywheel. GRIT takes and generates energy. Sure, it takes time to exercise. But exercise gives you energy, and energy makes you more productive and efficient, which saves you time. You have to schedule the time to invest some energy in order to gain more energy and greater GRIT.

GRIT GAINER™

T + E = M   Most students passively and half-heartedly put in long hours hacking away at their assignments, until, hopefully, they are finally complete. You can get two to three times more out of your day and your life if you apply the formula: Time + Energy = Momentum. Here's how:

1. Plan prime time. For any task that helps you achieve your goal (get in, get through, get out, get paid), schedule undistracted, focused time during the prime energy of your day. You'll get twice as much done in half the time.

2. Refuse distractions and temptations. Turn everything off. Lock yourself away. Be like a swimmer going the length of the pool underwater. Don't come up for air until you've touched the finish line and accomplished your task.

Putting It in Practice

THE GRIT ADVANTAGE

Successful time and energy management requires GRIT. Your path to success is in many ways simple. But that doesn't mean it's easy. If it were easy, a lot more people would fulfill their dreams.

At least once a week, if not every day or whenever you whip out your calendar to schedule something new, ask yourself this question to keep you on the gritty path to your success: "What adjustments can I make to make better use of my energy and time to fulfill my goals?"

Whenever you are confronted with a tempting choice, ask yourself, "If I spend my time and energy on this, will it help or hurt, accelerate or delay me fulfilling my goal?"

Is it a plus or a minus? Say yes to momentum. Say no to anything that slows you down. Expect it to be tough. Pause and appreciate when it's not. And know, the tougher it is, the more accomplished you'll feel.

HOW GRITTY ARE YOU?

Now that you've completed this chapter, how committed are you to:

1. Taking charge—owning your time, owning your schedule, and owning your decisions?

   Zero Commitment **0** —————————————————————————— **10** Fully Committed

2. Not letting distractions, excuses, laziness, or competing demands get in the way of what you need to do?

   Zero Commitment **0** —————————————————————————— **10** Fully Committed

3. Seeking advice on the stuff you don't know, so you avoid costly mistakes and wasted time?

   Zero Commitment **0** —————————————————————————— **10** Fully Committed

3 Money Management

Chapter goals to help you *get in, get through, get out, and get paid:*

In order to get in, get through, get out, and get paid, you will need to manage your finances effectively. Even though every college student has a unique financial situation, every student needs to become knowledgeable about money to be an effective money manager. Because college is a marathon and not a sprint, your ability to handle your financial resources effectively will ultimately determine if you have enough money to complete all of your required classes, graduate, and get started in your chosen career.

To meet those goals, *this chapter will help you:*

- Develop financial literacy
- Set financial goals
- Create strategies for managing your finances
- Evaluate the advantages and disadvantages of using credit
- Exercise "**smart GRIT**" to put your money to optimal use

MyStudentSuccessLab™

Log in to MyStudentSuccessLab.com to deepen your **GRIT** mindset and build the skills you'll need to get through the college experience.

Evan's Story

© MONKEY BUSINESS IMAGES/SHUTTERSTOCK

Evan felt he was on top of the world. At 20 years old, he had started college after working for two years after high school. He had real-life experience and a promising future ahead of him.

Although he missed out on scholarships, he had saved enough money to pay for the first two semesters and had also received a grant. He quit his full-time job so that he could concentrate on keeping his grades up.

What he didn't expect, however, were the extra costs of college—books, computers, and extra course materials.

"Have you ever worked for a moving company on the weekends?" he asked a classmate named Juanita.

"No, but I signed up for a research study with the psychology department. I made $50," she said.

"That would pay for that extra book that we have to buy in sociology. I didn't think we really had to have it," he said.

"I get everything on the syllabus—whether they mention it the first day of class or not," said Juanita.

Evan had been trying to get by without buying everything his professors had listed as required for the course. He had already missed some important assignments because he didn't have what he needed to do the work.

"The psych department has a sleep deprivation study; they will pay $120 to participants," Juanita said.

He definitely would be signing up.

Now, what do you think?

- What would you do if you were faced with unexpected college-related costs and the uncertainty of how to cover the added expenses?
  a. Worry a lot, but do little or nothing
  b. Talk to others about how I can earn more money to cover the additional costs
  c. Consider giving up on school, because I am already stressed about paying for it all
  d. Immediately sit down, revisit my budget, and look for ways to save and make more money

- To prepare for unexpected costs of your degree, what would you do?
  a. Take fewer hours so I can get a job to cover any unexpected expenses
  b. Research the potential additional costs that may be part of my degree in the next few semesters and find ways to cover them
  c. Seek out those who have been most successful with the financial struggles of school and adjust my approach accordingly
  d. Nothing; I can't predict or plan for the unknown

Budgeting your money for college expenses will be crucial to your staying in college and being less stressed.

© ROB MARMION/SHUTTERSTOCK

Financial Literacy Is a Lifelong Lesson

One of the greatest challenges for college students isn't meeting the academic expectations of college; it is handling the financial issues that come into play when you get there. Some students choose to go to school full time and not work, whereas others juggle a job—either part time or full time—while going to school. No matter what their financial situation, many are adding the expense of going to college to their other obligations, or they are using grants, loans, or scholarships to cover costs.

As you know by now, investing in your future takes more than courage; it also takes some cash. Unfortunately, the costs of college continue to rise and will likely increase with each passing year. So what can you do? The first step is to develop financial literacy. Financial literacy means that you have the working knowledge about finances that you need to make important decisions and the skills to effectively manage your financial resources. It's not enough to know a lot about money

You also need to apply that knowledge to your daily habits and choices. To get started, it's important to fully identify all of the costs that are associated with college and build a budget plan for managing your finances during your college years.

Estimate Your College Costs

Estimating what you are going to spend in college for your education is a great first step to becoming financially literate, and it will help you with budgeting. Because this is your first time in college, it will be helpful to see what you can expect to spend as you work on and complete your degree. The following is a common list of typical college expenses:

Instinct

Create a plan for your money and exercise the personal GRIT it takes to stick with it, despite any temptations to spend it on other things.

- **Fees and tuition.** This is what you pay for the classes you take. The amount you pay may vary based on the number of units you're taking, whether you are an in-state or out-of-state student, whether you are an undergraduate or graduate student, and perhaps even if you are in a specific major.

- **Books and supplies.** For most of the courses you take in college, you will be required to purchase a textbook, workbook, or other supplies. In college, you will be responsible for purchasing these items and bringing them to class. In addition to textbooks, you may also need to purchase notebooks, binders, a laptop or desktop computer, backpack, paper (for notes and for printing), pens and pencils, calculator, computer software, jump drive (for storing electronic files), stapler, hole punch, ruler, and other specialized supplies for labs or certain classes such as photography or drawing.

- **Room and board.** "Room" is the cost of your housing, either on campus in a dorm or off campus in an apartment. "Board" is the cost of your meals. If you choose to live in a dorm, you may have the option to purchase a meal plan that gives you a fixed amount of food each day at the various cafeterias across campus. If you live off campus, "board" would be the cost of groceries and restaurant charges.

- **Transportation.** Depending on your circumstances, you will have expenses associated with a vehicle, bicycle, or public transportation to get yourself from where you live to campus. You may also have fees for parking on campus.

- **Personal and miscellaneous.** This is a broad category of costs that includes movies and entertainment, clothing, your cell phone bill, magazine subscriptions, and other daily expenses—many of which are easy to forget unless you carefully track them.

You may also find other costs associated with going to college that aren't mentioned on your university's "cost of attendance" website or during new student orientation.

- **Insurance.** Depending on your circumstances, such as if you are not covered under your parents' medical insurance policy, you may need to pay for medical insurance, prescriptions, and medical costs not covered by insurance.

- **Internet.** You may also discover that you need regular, reliable Internet access that will create an additional monthly cost.

- **Child Care.** If you are raising a child while pursuing college, you may incur daycare or babysitting services.

Complete the Meeting Expectations exercise to begin thinking about what you can do to become financially literate.

Create a Budget

Once you've estimated all of the costs associated with college, you can build a monthly budget. A monthly budget is your plan for matching how much money you need with how much money you

It's in the
syllabus

Look at the syllabus for each of your courses to determine what additional costs you may have for each course. Be sure to consider possible unwritten costs such as the use of a computer, Internet, and printer.

- What textbook and course materials costs will you have?
- What technology costs will you have?
- What unwritten costs do you anticipate?
- How will budget and pay for these costs?

Meeting
expectations

The college will expect that I . . .	To meet that expectation, I will . . .
Example: . . . pay for all the costs of college as they come due.	*Example:*. . . research college material about cost estimates, talk to others in college to determine any "hidden" costs, and have a plan for having the money available when these costs are due.
_____	_____
_____	_____
_____	_____

Instinct

Be scrappy. Get gritty with your money by finding ways to get what you need for less. Some costs, like tuition, may be fixed. Some costs that appear fixed aren't. Shop the best deals and always ask for student discounts to get more for less.

have available. For this purpose, a budget has two main sections—income and expenses. The income section shows how much money you have available, either from a job, your savings, student loans, or other sources. The expense section shows your costs. Although it may seem obvious, the fundamental rule of a budget is that you can't spend more money than you have available. And because certain expenses like tuition and car insurance are due only a few times a year, you need to have a method for putting money aside so you have the funds available at a later date to pay these relatively large bills.

Once you have an estimate of all your anticipated costs, the process of building a monthly budget can be a relatively easy task. The hard part is following it. First, you need to create a customized budget sheet. In the first column, you will estimate your income and your expenses. The middle column will be used to track your actual income and expenses each month. Record any differences in the marked column by subtracting the actual amount from the estimated amount. For example, if you estimate that you earn about $1,000 a month, but this month, you earn $1,092, your difference is +$92. If you earned $997, then the difference is −$3. Comparing your budget plan to what's actually happening each month will help you make adjustments.

Once you determine the categories that fit your lifestyle and requirements, you will need to gather all the bills and paystubs that you have and add up your expenses and income. It is a good idea to review at least three months of bills to get an accurate picture of your expenditures. If you have any bills that are paid less frequently than once a month, then you will need to convert them to a monthly expense. For example, if you pay $240 for car insurance every six months, your monthly expense is $40 ($240 divided by 6).

One key to an accurate budget that helps you track your spending is to be honest about your expenses. That means you must write down everything you spend, even the money you spend on snacks or supplies. One method for tracking your spending is to save every receipt from every purchase, organize them by category, and total them each month. You may find that you spend $25 a week ($100 a month) on items that are unnecessary. The more you can track unnecessary items, the better you can control your spending.

Resilience

The fewer sources of income and the smaller the funds you have, the less resilient and the more vulnerable your situation becomes. If a lake is fed by one tributary, the lake is in danger when that creek dries up. If it is fed by two or more, its chances of survival dramatically improve. It may not be easy, but strive to create more than one source for your school funds. And whenever possible, build in a little padding, so you can weather the storm and stay in school.

Learn More about Your Finances

Financial literacy is a lifelong learning opportunity. You started learning some important lessons about money when you were very young and now you have a chance to learn even more by navigating the costs of college. There are numerous resources available for you to explore financial matters further. There are many local, state, and federal government programs that can provide free information and counseling if you are interested in getting your finances on track. Don't forget that your local library and bookstore offer many good resources on money management and financial matters.

Setting Financial Goals Will Help You Stay on Track

After you get an accurate picture of your income and expenses and you have a monthly budget plan, you can start setting short-term and long-term financial goals. Setting goals can help you fulfill your mission, live out your values, and achieve the success that defines your purpose. Financial goals are an important part of your personal plan because they help you determine if you're reaching the milestones you know are necessary to achieve long-term success.

Short-term goals should apply to the next 12 months of your life. For example, your first short-term goal could be tracking your monthly budget and consistently spending 5 percent less than you earn. Another short-term goal could be to put enough money in your savings account each month to pay for your study abroad experience next year. Because your budget is the product of both income and expenses, your short-term goals might apply to either. For example, if you want to have $1,000 in savings by next summer to buy a new computer, you could set short-term goals for both earning extra income and reducing your expenses.

Your long-term goals apply to your future in the next two to five years and beyond. Long-term goals can be an extension of your short-term goals. For example, you may set a long-term goal to pay for college without having to take out any student loans. Your long-term goal of avoiding student loans can only be attained if you can achieve your short-term goal of keeping your expenses below your income every month.

Financial goals are an important part of your personal plan and mission, and they can serve as useful guides and powerful motivators to help you make the decisions day after day and week after week that are necessary to their achievement.

Complete Activity 3.1, Setting SMART Financial Goals, to write out some of your financial goals.

■ There are so many scholarships that go unclaimed each year. Look for ones that you qualify for and apply!

> ### ■ ACTIVITY 3.1   Setting SMART Financial Goals
>
> Use the SMART approach (specific, measurable, achievable, realistic, time-specific) to write financial goals for your first term, your first year, and for all four years of your college experience. Then, identify someone with whom you can share these goals, discuss them, and help you stay on track to achieve them.

A Good Strategy Can Help You Manage Your Finances

A good financial plan is only good if you stick to it. The following tips can help you increase your financial literacy muscles, especially if you exercise them regularly:

- **Balance your checkbook and other accounts every month.** Online tools like Quicken and Mint.com can be helpful, if you're comfortable managing your finances using a computer.

If you're just getting started, a simple tool like an Excel spreadsheet or a paper-and-pencil monthly budget tracking form might be a great choice.

- **Compare your bank's financial statements with your own recording of expenses and income.** This will help you catch any unauthorized charges on your accounts or bank fees that were inappropriately posted to your account.

- **Separate your bills from other mail and create a schedule for paying them.** Your paper-based or electronic calendar system is ideal for this purpose. Most bills are due on the same day each month, so you can set up a recurring reminder.

- **Sign up for online payment plans if available and if it is easier to pay this way.** Just be sure that you have reliable Internet access and use a consistent email address so you don't lose track of these transactions.

- **If you have a credit card, use it for emergencies only.** Resist the temptation to use your credit card for everyday expenses.

- **Put a small percentage of your income each month in a separate savings account for unexpected expenses.** For example, for every $100 you earn, put $5 (5%) in an emergency savings account. Create a goal to increase your savings percentage over time.

the unwritten rules
of Money Management

- **Loans will often be included in your college's financial aid "offer" to you; just remember that loans will need to be paid back.** Sometimes, a financial aid package or offer will seem to appear as if you are paying very little out of your pocket for college. Look carefully to see what part of the costs is being covered by loans, because that's the part you'll have to pay back—with interest.

- **More academic options are emerging in higher education.** With your academic plan in hand and full knowledge of the courses you need to take to complete your degree, be a savvy customer and be aware of your options for how to earn that credit. For example, if you are attending a four-year university, a local community college may offer general education courses available online or over the summer that are acceptable substitutes for courses at your university.

- **Make every course count!** If your college budget is tight, you need to make sure that every course you take will apply towards your degree progress. Sometimes students will pick up extra classes because they didn't like the time or day when the class they needed for their degree was offered.

- **The best paying college jobs are sometimes the least glamorous.** College students are sometimes attracted to high visibility jobs like bartending in a popular hangout or merchandising in the trendiest clothing store. Meanwhile, there may be jobs in your area that pay a lot more and offer better experience, but aren't perceived as popular or cool. Distribution centers, daycares, cleaning and maintenance firms, local factories, or telephone-based customer service positions may be advertised in the "help wanted" or "temporary hire" sections of the want ads or via a temp agency in your area.

- **Check the university's website every semester for updates about changes in tuition and fees.** Keep yourself informed about expected expenses from semester to semester.
- **Use the National Student Loan Data System website.** This website will help you keep track of all your federal financial aid so you know what you owe when you graduate (https://www.nslds.ed.gov).

Protect Yourself

Budgeting and creating a plan are not quite enough to make sure that you are on firm financial foundation—you will also need to protect yourself from scams, which can do more harm than just draining your bank account. If the information sounds too good to be true or doesn't seem right, it is quite possibly a scam.

Another risk that you have to manage is identity theft. Keep your bank cards in a safe, secure place at all time, and never, ever write down your ATM PIN on a piece of paper. Also, be very cautious any time someone asks you to provide your Social Security number. Never provide it in an email, and make sure that any form requesting this number is from an official authority like your college's financial aid office or the registrar.

Tenacity

Most students end up spending money on things they don't need. The harder you work, the more tempting it becomes to buy yourself little indulgences along the way. If cash is tight, use your GRIT to focus your funds on what matters most. It will save you money and enhance your sense of accomplishment.

There Are Advantages and Disadvantages of Using Credit

There are generally two reasons why college students use credit cards instead of cash or checks to purchase items. The first reason is that they don't have enough money to afford the purchase. The second reason is that credit cards are a convenient form of payment. Students who rely on credit cards to make up for a lack of available funds tend to find themselves in financial trouble very quickly because credit cards typically carry high interest rates and students have a tough time earning enough income to pay off accumulating debt. If you charge $1,000 on a credit card that charges 17 percent interest, and you make payments of $100 each month, you will be accruing more in interest than you will be paying each month. And that is only if you do not charge anything else!

If you are attracted to a credit card because of its convenience, check with your current bank about the availability of a debit card. A debit card offers the same convenience as a credit card, but the funds for each purchase are withdrawn from your checking account, rather than loaned to you on credit. This distinctive feature of debit cards can help you avoid getting into the debt and high interest charges that have shipwrecked many students.

You Have Options for Paying for College

When thinking about your financial future, most likely paying for college will be at the top of your list. Even if you have a solid plan for paying for tuition, fees, and books, it will be worth your time to investigate other methods in case your current plan falls through.

Scholarships

Winning a scholarship is by far the most rewarding (financially and psychologically) way to pay for college because it is literally free money—you don't have to pay it back. There are thousands of scholarships available for needy and accomplished students, but you often have to work hard to find them. To find the ones that match your profile, you will need to get the word out to friends and family that you are looking.

Another way to get information about scholarships is to talk with the financial aid officers and counselors at your college. They have access to and knowledge of scholarships that fit the college's student profiles, such as single-parent and transfer scholarships that will pay your tuition and fees at a four-year university. Other effective methods for finding scholarships are to investigate sources at your library and search the Internet. Searching print and web-based databases will provide you with more than enough information, but you'll need to narrow your focus so you can locate the options that best fit your qualities and circumstances.

Whatever information about scholarships you find—whether it's in books, in counselors' offices, or on the Internet—don't pay for it. No reputable scholarship will require that you pay a fee to apply, and very few scholarship services will require payment. There are legitimate scholarship searching services out there, but be careful. The website FinAid! (www.finaid.org) provides information about different types of financial aid for college students, as well as tips for avoiding scholarship services scams.

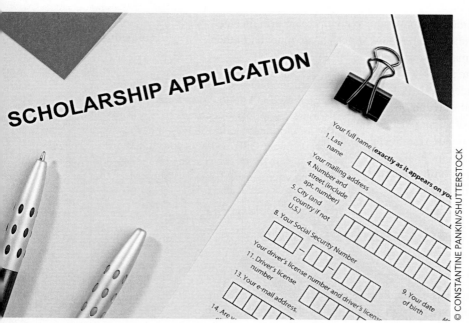

■ Being able to finance your college degree will help you achieve your dreams.

Grants

By definition, grants are a form of financial assistance that does not need to be paid back. A common federal grant is the Pell Grant, which can be awarded for full-time or part-time enrollment. To determine your eligibility, talk with your financial aid counselor or visit any of the various websites that provide governmental information about financial aid. When you research Pell Grants, you will find that there is a maximum to the amount of the award ($5,500 for 2014–2015) and that your college will receive the money and then disburse it to you once classes start. Because of recent federal requirements about grants and student loans, colleges may wait several weeks before paying students. If you are expecting to receive your grant the first day or week of classes, you should make alternative arrangements to pay bills (including your bookstore bill). The Lifetime Eligibility Used (LEU) for Pell Grants is 600 percent of the maximum that you qualify for. For example, if you quality for $4,000 per year, your LEU is $24,000. Once you meet your LEU, you are no longer eligible for Pell Grants.

Another type of grant that a student can receive is the Federal Supplemental Educational Opportunity Grant (FSEOG), which is available to those who demonstrate an exceptional need. According to the U.S. Department of Education, the difference between a Pell Grant and an FSEOG is that "each participating school will receive enough money to pay the Federal Pell Grants of its eligible students. There's no guarantee every eligible student will be able to receive an FSEOG." The procedure for receiving an FSEOG is similar to that for receiving a Pell Grant; your eligibility will determine the amount that you receive, and your college will disburse the money to you after the semester begins.

You will need to maintain good academic standing at your college to remain eligible for a grant, so be sure to make note of the minimum GPA that you must maintain to receive future grant money. One last tip for continuing to receive grant funding: Make sure that you adhere to the college's attendance policy. You may be penalized (and lose your grant funding or have to pay it back) for missing too many classes or for dropping a class.

Student Loans

In the event that you are not eligible for grants, or if they aren't enough to cover all your costs, you should investigate student loans. The idea of taking out a loan to attend college makes many students shudder with fear because they don't want the added pressure that they must pay back what they borrow. If you can avoid a student loan, then by all means do so. However, receiving a student loan sometimes makes more financial sense in the long run, if the alternative is to forgo college.

> **G R I T**
> **Tenacity**
>
> Take a gritty approach to applying for loans and scholarship grants by applying for a variety of different ones, making sure you complete all the steps, following up, and being persistent in each step of the process until you get what you need. Persistence pays off when it comes to financial aid.

Federal student loans are typically low interest and can be paid back over 10 years. For families that would otherwise have to deplete their savings or borrow against retirement or their mortgages to pay for college, a low-interest student loan is a good option. Most loan programs allow you to defer (which means to delay) payment until after you graduate; you can sometimes continue to defer payment if you remain unemployed after you graduate. However, these loans may accumulate interest during this deferral period, so be sure to know the specific terms of your loan before making decisions.

One type of loan is the Stafford Loan, which comes in subsidized and unsubsidized versions. A subsidized loan is one in which the government pays the interest for you while you are in college. Once you graduate and start making payments on your loan, you will accrue interest as well. The government does not make interest payments for an unsubsidized loan, so you would need to decide whether to pay the interest while you are in college (usually a small amount), or allow the interest to be added (or capitalized) to the overall loan amount and wait until after you graduate to make any payments. This is a classic "pay now or pay more later" type of decision that you need to carefully evaluate.

A federal Perkins Loan is a loan between you and your college. The Perkins Loan currently allows you to borrow $5,500 per year, up to $27,500 for five years, and you don't have to start to repay it until nine months after you graduate or drop below at least part-time status (Student Aid on the Web, 2014). One benefit of a Perkins Loan is that you may be able to cancel up to 100 percent of the debt if you meet certain criteria. For example, upon graduation, if you choose to teach in a "teacher shortage" area, or if you serve as a full-time nurse, you may be eligible for cancellation of your loan.

PLUS, which stands for Parent Loan for Undergraduate Students, is another method for receiving money to help pay for college. If you are fortunate enough to have parents willing to take out a loan to help you pay for college, a PLUS is a possible option. To qualify, you must be a dependent student, which means your parents support you financially. Parents who take out a PLUS are usually trying to make up the difference between the cost of tuition and the financial aid package that their children receive. Nonetheless, it is the parents who are ultimately responsible for repaying the loan, which can begin as early as 60 days after they receive it.

GRIT GAINER™

YES AND NO   One of the most powerful ways to get gritty with your money is to make a list of those things that are utterly required to fulfill your goal of getting in, through, out, and paid. Ask yourself, "What is the minimum amount of money it takes for me to have/buy each of these items?" List those numbers. Say "yes!" to those items.

Next, make a list of all the things you know you spend money on that you do not absolutely need. You may really want them, but that doesn't mean you need them. Every dollar wasted on a want is a dollar less to nurture your needs. Say "no" to those items, at least more often than you do now.

THE GRIT ADVANTAGE

Imagine your best friend was applying to college, and he or she was going to be very tight on funds. If your friend asked you to map out and teach him or her how to manage his or her money while in college, specifically, what would you tell your friend to do? Based on everything you learned in this chapter, what are three things you'd want your friend to be sure to do, and three things not to do, in order to increase the chances of remaining financially solid?

Now—apply your own advice.

HOW GRITTY ARE YOU?

Now that you've completed this chapter, how committed are you to:

1. Planning and managing your money so you can reduce your stress and enhance your college experience?

   Zero Commitment 0 —————————————————————————— 10 Fully Committed

2. Demonstrating the personal discipline to spend your money on things related to your goals and not waste it on things unrelated to your goals?

   Zero Commitment 0 —————————————————————————— 10 Fully Committed

3. Taking charge of your financial situation and asking advice from students who have successfully managed their money through college?

   Zero Commitment 0 —————————————————————————— 10 Fully Committed

4 Critical and Creative Thinking

Chapter goals to help you *get in, get through, get out, and get paid:*

As you set your sights on getting in, getting through, getting out, and getting paid, your ability to think critically and creatively will help you every step of the way. Critical and creative thinking will be an important tool in your toolbox for the rest of your life.

To meet those goals, *this chapter will help you:*

- Develop critical thinking skills
- Practice creative thinking techniques
- Appreciate the value of using critical, analytical, and creative thinking skills to solve problems better and faster
- Apply **GRIT** to think through and solve problems more effectively

MyStudentSuccessLab™

Log in to MyStudentSuccessLab.com to deepen your **GRIT** mindset and build the skills you'll need to get through the college experience.

Michael's Story

© MONKEY BUSINESS IMAGES/SHUTTERSTOCK

Michael can hike 12 miles in a hot sandstorm with 30 pounds of equipment on his back. What Michael can't do, he believes, is understand algebra.

Inside the student center, Michael sits back down on a chair and opens his math notebook.

"The order of operations is F-O-I-L: first, outer, inner, last. But after that, I don't know what to do," he thinks to himself.

If his professor would just slow down and allow students to get it before moving on to the next unit, he wouldn't feel so stressed.

"Isn't teaching me algebra *his* job, not a tutor's?" Michael asks.

Michael finds it difficult to seek help on his own. By the time he got to high school, he was able to slide by, and in the military his superiors ordered everything he did.

Before he decides to leave, his girlfriend Michelle calls him.

"Michael, do you remember when I struggled through biology? I wanted to be a nurse so much, but I struggled," she says.

"Yeah, I do. I remember helping you study before tests."

"Do you remember how much better I did after I went to the tutoring center? I found someone who helped me take better notes."

"You're right," Michael says. "I need to get over myself and see what kind of help I can get."

Michael walks into the tutoring center.

Now, what do you think?

- If you found yourself struggling in a class, what would you do?
  a. Worry about my ability to succeed, but keep doing what I have always done
  b. Find someone to help me because I know that I cannot do it all by myself
  c. Just try harder

- If you were uncomfortable asking for help when you need it, what would you do?
  a. Nothing; it is not someone else's responsibility to help me succeed
  b. Approach it carefully, find the most comfortable way to get some initial help, and then ask for more help if I need it
  c. Put aside my ego and ask anyway

Critical Thinking Skills Will Serve You Well

Strong critical thinking skills will set you apart in the classroom and the workplace: You will be better informed, because you will know how to find the information you need; you will make better choices, because you will understand your alternatives and their trade-offs; and you will continue to improve your decisions over time by learning from each new experience.

A critical thinker is "someone who uses specific criteria to evaluate reasoning and make decisions" (Diestler, 1998, p. 2). Someone who thinks critically does not take information at its face value; instead, he or she carefully examines information for accuracy, authority, and logic before using it.

To illustrate the importance of using critical thinking skills, consider this first scenario: Michael receives an email from a friend who claims that she has sent him a virus unknowingly. Her message instructs him to search for the offending file and delete it immediately. Unaware of any problems that are usually associated with viruses, he searches for the file and finds it, exactly where his friend said it would be on his computer. Michael's friend is a trustworthy person and he values her advice, so he deletes the file. He gets an email the next day from her that says she is sorry that the previous email she sent him was actually a hoax. Thus, he has deleted a perfectly normal file on his computer.

Now, consider this second scenario: Juanita sends Evan a link to a pop-up blocker because she knows that he hates those annoying intrusions while surfing the Internet. Because Evan has been deceived by free software before, he

Finding and using resources on the Internet provides great opportunities for you to practice good critical thinking skills.

© AUREMAR/SHUTTERSTOCK

decides to search several reputable sites that are devoted to reviewing new software. Evan finds that the pop-up blocker is a fraud; instead, if he were to click on the link that Juanita has sent, his computer would have been overrun with pop-up advertisements of questionable origins.

In the first scenario, two people, at least, have been deceived by what appears to be legitimate and helpful information. Who doesn't want to rid their computer of a potentially dangerous virus? Unfortunately, Michael and his friend did not question the information. In the second scenario, however, Evan has encountered false claims before and realizes that he must check out every piece of information that comes to him, regardless of the friendly source. Evan applied critical thinking to the situation. Thinking critically allowed him to review the information he was sent and search for authoritative sources that provided reliable information so that he could make a decision about what action to take.

The two scenarios demonstrate the importance of critical thinking skills and how you can develop and practice these skills for yourself. To think critically, you need to look for information that supports your own ideas and solutions and, with equal openness, look for information that supports ideas and solutions that are different than your own. One of the best illustrations of critical thinking is a voter's guide. Exhibit 4.1 shows a section from the June 2014 California voter's guide pertaining to Proposition 41. The guide explains what Proposition 41 means and provides statements both in support (pro), and against (con) the proposition. The guide also points to additional sources of information pertaining to both the pro argument and the con argument. The information in this voter's guide is purposely intended to foster critical thinking. Voters who take the time to carefully review information on both sides of an argument are practicing critical thinking because they are carefully evaluating both perspectives before making a final decision.

Critical thinking skills, therefore, include the ability to identify your question or problem and to seek information from several sources and points of view before making a decision or drawing a conclusion.

To practice critical thinking skills and develop your ability to think critically, be on the lookout for situations where different perspectives or points of view might lead to new ideas or different conclusions. These situations might occur in class, in a club or Greek organizational activity, at work, with your roommates, or at home with your family.

It's in the
syllabus

As you review the detailed contents of the syllabus from each class you are taking this semester, you'll find many places where critical thinking skills will be important:

- Will there be multiple-choice questions on quizzes and tests that will challenge you to critically evaluate each answer option to select the "best" answer?
- Will you have term papers and reports that will challenge you to find reliable sources of information that support your ideas?
- Can you find at least two other examples from your course syllabi that require critical thinking?

GRIT
Growth

Change your angle on the problem. A key element of GRIT is mental agility. This means looking at problems from fresh perspectives, with fresh ideas and fresh eyes. Ask yourself, "How would the world's greatest problem solver, who knows nothing about this situation, approach this problem?"

Meeting
expectations

The college will expect that I . . .	To meet that expectation, I will . . .
Example: . . . demonstrate critical thinking skills in my classes and in every aspect of my college life.	*Example:* . . . gather and study information that will help me to evaluate my own beliefs and conclusions, and the beliefs and conclusions of others.
_____	_____
_____	_____
_____	_____

EXHIBIT 4.1 Proposition 41 Pro and Con

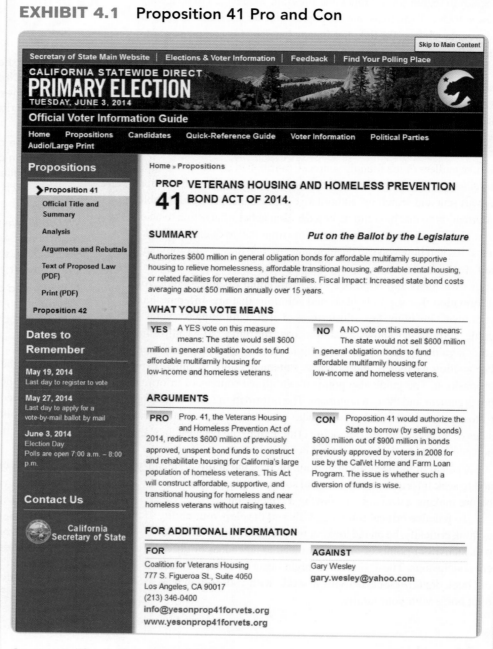

Source: California Secretary of State.

■ ACTIVITY 4.1 Critical Thinking in Action

Write down three examples of situations that you can expect to encounter during your first term in college when you could practice critical thinking. For example, are there topics that you will study in some of your classes that might generate debate or disagreement between you and your professor or classmates? For each of the three examples, briefly describe how you could actively demonstrate critical thinking.

Creative Thinking Helps You Develop New Ideas

Creative thinking, or the act of creating ideas for solving problems, is an integral part of learning. Without creative thinking, there would be no inventions, new formulas, breakthroughs in technology and science, new art movements, advances in design and architecture—the list is endless. Without creative thinking, there would be no electricity, no indoor plumbing, no automobiles, and no zippers in our clothes. Just getting to your classes would be a totally different experience.

Creative thinking is more than a process for generating ideas; it is an attitude and a skill that can be developed over time. In other words, creative thinkers are not born with special powers of the imagination; they just use their imaginations more regularly than others. The good news is that you can learn to think creatively by following some of the basic ideas shown in Exhibit 4.2.

Use the questions in Exhibit 4.2 to generate creative uses for a paperclip, candle, and penny:

_____

_____

_____

_____

_____

Robert Harris states in his book *Creative Thinking Helps You Build Ideas*, "Creative thinking creates the ideas with which critical thinking works" (Harris, 2002, p. 202). To improve your creative abilities, practice the ideas described in Exhibit 4.3, maintain your curiosity about new ideas and perspectives, and spend time with people who have different backgrounds, experiences, and perspectives than your own.

Critical and Creative Thinking Skills Can Help You Solve Problems

Although not all critical thinking leads to solving a problem, problem solving relies on critical thinking, as well as creative and analytical thinking. In order to think critically to solve a problem, you will need to go through a process within a group or as an individual. Remember that the more minds are working on a problem, the more likely that all sides of the problem can be addressed, which may make the solution better. You may not always have an opportunity to work in a group on a problem, but you may be able to ask others for their advice during the process.

> Guess what predicts who solves problems better and faster than everyone else? *GRIT*. Research shows that as you grow and show your GRIT, you will be even more innovative and work through sticky problems more quickly and effectively.

Once you have your gritty mindset in place, here are the basic steps for using critical thinking to solve a problem:

- Clearly identify the problem or goal.
- Generate several possible solutions to the problem or goal.
- Critically evaluate each possible solution.
- Choose one of the solutions and develop a plan for putting it in action.
- Evaluate the solution after it is in place.

EXHIBIT 4.2 Questions to Generate Ideas

How can it be put to another use?

How can it be changed?

What could you take away from it?

What could you add to it?

EXHIBIT 4.3   Creative Thinking Strategies, Definitions, and Activities

Strategy	Definition	Activity
Try to improve your imagination each day.	Find ways to keep your mind sharp and your imagination flourishing. Turning off the TV and picking up a book is an easy way to stimulate your imagination. If you enjoy kinesthetic activities, create something to get your mind active.	Participate in one thinking or imaginative exercise each day, whether it's doing a crossword puzzle or Sudoku puzzle, constructing an object, or listing the plusses and minuses of the healthiness of what you ate for breakfast.
Consider what someone else would do.	Looking at a problem from a different perspective can provide you with more creative ideas.	Determine what topic or problem you want to generate more ideas for. Then choose two people—such as your mother and perhaps Oprah Winfrey or Walt Disney—and write down the different ways they would approach the issue.
Hold off on making judgments.	For creative thinking, evaluating or judging isn't necessary. Save it for critical thinking and problem solving.	Make a list of 50 ways to use a paper clip, and don't delete items or edit the list in any way. Share your list with others.

■ Creative and critical thinking are both important skills that will help you solve problems and create new solutions.

© HASLOO GROUP PRODUCTION STUDIO/SHUTTERSTOCK

Exhibit 4.3 provides more information about incorporating creative thinking into your everyday practice.

Step 1: Identify the Problem or Goal

Sometimes a problem is obvious, and other times we may make an incorrect assumption about the real problem. Either way, it's important to take some time to clearly identify the problem before moving on to possible solutions. For example, if you're constantly late for your first class every morning, you might assume it's because you're not getting up early enough. After examining the situation more closely, however, you discover that you're spending too much time trying to find a parking spot before class. The problem may actually be a transportation problem and not a problem with your sleeping habits. Or, instead of a problem, we may be trying to accomplish a particular goal. For example, you might set a goal to save an extra $200 over the next six months so you can buy an ebook reader.

Identifying the problem's cause is the first logical step before you can begin to solve it. If you do not identify the cause—or at least eliminate possible causes—before starting the next step, either you won't solve the problem or you might create a whole new problem to solve.

Step 2: Generate Possible Solutions

This is the step where creative thinking will kick in. When you generate ideas, there are no rules except not to eliminate any ideas because they are too far-fetched or too odd. The goal for this step is to get a lot of ideas on paper. The more ideas you can think of, the more likely you'll come up with a really creative solution that comes from "outside the box"—a phrase that describes ideas that aren't readily obvious.

When generating ideas, consider creating a list of your possible ideas and role playing (if you are able to work with another person) to get ideas flowing. This is a good time to take advantage of your learning style strength to stretch your imagination. For the "late for class" problem, you might identify some obvious solutions (e.g., riding your bike to class instead of driving), but by giving yourself room to be really creative and open, you might come up with some less-than-obvious ideas, like packing your breakfast in a cooler and eating it *after* you find a parking spot (which doesn't fix the parking problem, but helps resolve the overall problem of arriving late to class by saving you time each morning).

Step 3: Critically Evaluate Each Possible Solution

To critically evaluate means that you consider the advantages and disadvantages, strengths and weaknesses, plusses and minuses of every option. Sometimes it's helpful to construct a chart or table that describes each solution in the first column, the advantages, strengths, and plusses in the second column, and the disadvantages, weaknesses, and minuses in the third column. It's helpful to force yourself to fill in every square in the grid so that you are thorough in considering both sides of a solution, especially if you find yourself preferring one particular solution from the very beginning. This is also a time when the opinions of others can be very helpful. Your friends, parents, professors, and roommates can provide a critical perspective that can help you understand your options better than you could have done yourself. For example, if you're considering the possibility of getting a part-time job to make the money you want to save for your ebook reader, your trusted advisors might help you discover some of the drawbacks of adding work to your weekly schedule because of their own personal experiences with similar circumstances.

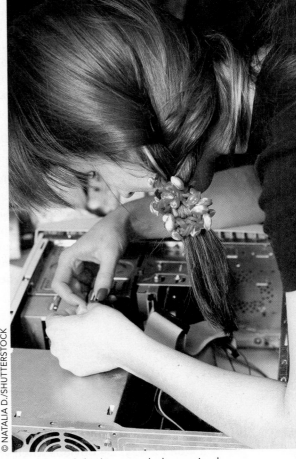

© NATALIA D./SHUTTERSTOCK

Analytical thinking can help you in classes that require you to learn processes.

Step 4: Select and Implement Your Solution

Some people have a tendency to make decisions too quickly before giving careful consideration to all the possible alternatives and potential outcomes. Other people, however, spend too much time considering all the alternatives and agonizing over the possible outcomes, and they have trouble making a final decision. The best course of action, of course, is to be somewhere in the middle—giving careful thought to each potential solution and then making a final decision in a timely manner. Once you've carefully evaluated all of your possible solutions, you eventually need to make a decision.

G R I T
Tenacity

Gritty problem solvers become excavators. They dig underneath by asking, "What's the problem underneath this problem (or the issue underneath this issue)?" Getting to the bedrock will help you build a solution that stands strong.

Evaluate each possible solution based on its plusses and minuses, pick the one that has the most plusses compared to minuses, and then move on to put the solution into action. It's one thing to decide to do something, but it's a far different step to put that decision into action. If you chose riding your bike to class as your solution to getting to class on time in the morning, you need to have a bike with a lock and know where you can park it near your classroom. You might also need to make a test run on a day when you don't have class to figure out how long it will take to get to your class using a different mode of transportation.

Step 5: Evaluate the Solution

This is one of the easiest steps to overlook, and yet it's one of the most important. You can become a more effective problem solver and decision maker by revisiting the decisions you've made in the past and evaluating how they turned out in the long run. By examining several decisions over a six-month or one-year period, you'll see patterns, and, if you practice the problem-solving process described here, you'll see a gradual, steady improvement in your decision making and problem solving over time. By practicing this five-step process on a regular basis with relatively simple problems, you'll develop effective skills to tackle the really big problems when they arise. You'll have a lifelong habit that will serve you well.

the unwritten rules
about Critical and Creative Thinking

- **It won't always be obvious when you will need to practice critical thinking.** You'll need to be an alert and vigilant information processor when you're in college, and almost every decision you face will require careful consideration and a gritty response. For example, during a meeting with your study group, one of your classmates might tell you that the exam will only cover the first five chapters of the textbook. You may not want to take one person's opinion at face value in this kind of situation, because the consequences would be significant. If you walk into class on exam day and discover that Chapters 6 and 7 were also on the test, you'll have no one to blame but yourself.

- **Too much stress, fatigue, and time pressure can kill creativity.** A little bit of stress might help to get you motivated, but too much of it will typically cause you to shut down. If you have a project or assignment that requires creative thinking, it's best to give yourself some time to work on the project in advance. Some research suggests that your mind actually develops creative solutions when you're asleep, so give yourself a few days to generate ideas before the project deadline.

- **Some of your best ideas will come when you least expect them.** Successful entrepreneurs and inventors often refer to thoughts that occur to them while they're in the shower or when they are engaged in an activity completely unrelated to the problem they're trying to solve. Keep a notepad and pencil handy wherever you are so that you can put your ideas on paper when they occur, and you reduce the chances of forgetting really good ideas when they come.

- **Failure and mistakes can help you become a better thinker.** Some students are so focused on getting perfect scores and all A's that they resist taking chances that might lead to failure. This approach might lead to a high GPA, but it can stifle your ability to generate creative solutions. If you make mistakes or fail, review the circumstances and your decision making process, and use the experience to help you generate new ideas and solutions.

GRIT GAINER™

SLOW DOWN TO SPEED UP Problem solving requires you to really pause, focus, think, analyze, and solve. Go beyond "good enough" and strive for the best possible solution, especially on the ones that count, by asking yourself these questions:

1. What would be an even better way to solve this problem?

2. If I had to solve it faster and/or more completely, how would I do it?

3. If there were a tougher but better option, what might it be?

Take It with You

Action Item	Deadline	First Step
Anticipate circumstances when critical thinking will be needed.		
Develop effective creative thinking habits and routines.		
Practice the five-step problem solving process.		

Putting It in Practice

THE GRIT ADVANTAGE

Research shows that GRIT is the single most important factor when it comes to optimizing your creative and critical thinking. Challenge yourself with these questions to fortify your GRIT mindset and put this chapter into practice:

1. Based on all you've learned in this chapter, what is the one thing you would benefit from the most and might need to work hard to master?

2. How can you use the tools presented in this chapter to approach things more creatively?

3. What is one specific problem you'd like to solve more creatively and/or effectively?

4. Of all the tools/tips offered, which one do you commit to use first?

HOW GRITTY ARE YOU??

Now that you've completed this chapter, how committed are you to:

1. Applying these techniques to become a more critical thinker?

Zero Commitment 0 ———————————————————— 10 Fully Committed

2. Applying these tools to think more creatively?

Zero Commitment 0 ———————————————————— 10 Fully Committed

3. Applying these tools to solve problems more effectively?

Zero Commitment 0 ———————————————————— 10 Fully Committed

5 Learning Preferences

Chapter goals to help you
get in,
get through,
get out,
and get paid:

An important part of the college experience is to learn more about yourself. The more you know about yourself, the better you'll be able to tackle the challenges and pursue the opportunities that lie ahead. This chapter is designed to help you understand yourself better, particularly your learning style and preferences.

To meet those goals, this chapter will help you:

- Describe different learning preferences
- Determine your learning preferences
- Use classroom and study strategies for different learning preferences
- Explore major and career options for different learning preferences
- Tap your **GRIT** to apply these tools to become a better, grittier learner

MyStudentSuccessLab

Log in to MyStudentSuccessLab.com to deepen your **GRIT** mindset and build the skills you'll need to get through the college experience.

Four Student Stories: Orientation

BOTTOM RIGHT: © ANDRESR/SHUTTERSTOCK
ALL OTHERS: © MONKEY BUSINESS IMAGES/SHUTTERSTOCK

"Destination: Degree," the travel-themed orientation, is winding down after an afternoon of skits, presentations, and door prizes.

"If everyone will score their inventories, we will explain how learning style preference affects your study habits," says Jason, an orientation leader.

"Hey, I am 'kinesthetic.' That kind of makes sense. I teach kickboxing and learned how to do it by working out almost every day," Evan says.

"I thought I would be more of a social learner, but my learning style preference is 'individual,'" says Michael as he rubs his head. "I spent so much time leading troops when I was in the military."

"I am definitely 'auditory,'" Laura says to the group. "I got through all my classes in high school by listening to the lectures. I rarely took notes because I liked to listen."

"Yeah, I can see that. You talked during every presentation!" Evan jokes.

"Will you be able to do that in college, just listen?" Juanita, the youngest of the group, asks. "I mean, I have heard that the professors expect so much more of you when it comes to being in class."

"I am sure you will," says Michael. "My girlfriend graduated last year with a degree in nursing. All she did was read for class and then study her notes every night."

"I know Laura is the talkative one, but give me a call if you ever need anything. Good luck to everyone!" Jason says.

Now, what do you think?

- How would you use information about your learning style preferences?
  a. Nothing; I don't have much faith that they can be helpful to me
  b. Learn more about my learning style preferences and find a way to use them to my advantage
  c. Avoid classes and instructors who do not play to my strengths
  d. Intentionally take on challenging learning situations so I can expand my abilities

- Do you see a learning style preference helping you in group situations?
  a. Most definitely; knowing everyone's learning style preferences can help us
  b. Not really. It may help me when I am by myself, but not when I am working with others.
  c. Only in certain circumstances when I know what everyone's learning preference is.

There Are Different Types of Intelligence

Have you ever admired someone else's achievements and wished you could be that smart or talented? Do you think you have to be either "book smart" or athletic to achieve? Although you may think there is only one or two ways to be smart or talented, there are actually several ways that you can learn. Consider how you fit into the following categories of intelligence, which were developed by Harvard psychologist Howard Gardner:

■ Kinesthetic learning involves using your hands and body to master a concept.

© LAYLAND MASUDA/SHUTTERSTOCK

- **Verbal/linguistic intelligence** is evident in people who can use language with ease. People who demonstrate verbal/linguistic intelligence enjoy reading and writing and may be journalists, novelists, playwrights, or comedians.

- **Logical/mathematical intelligence** is demonstrated by an ease and enjoyment with numbers and logic problems. People who have a strong leaning toward logical/mathematical intelligence like to solve problems, find patterns, discover relationships between objects, and follow steps. Career choices for logical/ mathematical people include science, computer technology, math, and engineering.

- **Visual/spatial intelligence** is characterized by anything visual, such as paintings, photographs, maps, and architecture. People who have a strong visual/spatial sense are usually good at design, architecture, painting and sculpture, and map making.

- **Body/kinesthetic intelligence** focuses on movement. Body/kinesthetic people enjoy using their bodies to express themselves. Obvious career choices for this intelligence include dancing, sports, and dramatic arts.

- **Musical/rhythmic intelligence** is a proficiency with musical rhythm and hearing tones and beats. People who have strong musical/rhythmic intelligence may use musical instruments or the human voice to express themselves. Career choices for this intelligence include all types of musical performers.

- **Interpersonal intelligence** is an ability to relate well with others. People with this intelligence read others' feelings well and act with others in mind.

- **Intrapersonal intelligence** is centered around the ability to understand oneself. People who possess intrapersonal intelligence know how and why they do what they do.

- **Naturalistic intelligence** refers to people who enjoy and work well in an outdoor environment. Naturalistic people find peace in nature and enjoy having natural elements around them.

GRIT
Growth

Don't settle for or accept labels. Most intelligences are not fixed. Gritty learners seek to grow in new ways, expanding their intelligences and capacities.

■ **ACTIVITY 5.1**   **Reflection on Multiple Intelligences**

As you read about these various types of intelligence, which ones tend to describe you best? How could understanding this about yourself help you better succeed in college?

Different Theories Provide Unique Insights

There are numerous ways to see yourself and understand your behavior in certain situations, and many education specialists and psychologists have provided theories on how we take in and process information. They have developed different inventories and personality profiles to enhance your understanding of yourself. As you will discover, the learning process is somewhat complex and involves more than just our preferences in how we create knowledge; there are many factors that influence our ability to take in and process information.

Theories about how the brain works have also given us insight into how people think, learn, and see the world. Some researchers make a distinction between the left side of the brain and the right side, suggesting that people who have strong left-brain tendencies are more likely to be logical, to see the parts rather than the whole, and to prefer to do activities step by step. They are also more analytical, realistic, and verbal than their right-brained companions. The right-brain preference is to see the whole picture rather than the details, to work out of sequence, and to bring ideas together.

Other researchers suggest that the real distinction is between the top and bottom parts of the brain, and that different people use these two parts to different degrees. The top-brain system draws on information from the surrounding environment to set goals and make plans. The bottom-brain system draws on signals from the senses and compares them to information stored in memory to interpret objects or events and to give them meaning.

The Myers-Briggs Type Indicator® (MBTI®) is an example of a personality assessment that also provides you with information about how you prefer to think and act. For example, one dimension of the

It's in the
syllabus

Your professors' syllabi contain clues about how the content will address learning style preferences. For example, a syllabus for biology may include a description of a kinesthetic class project that will involve creating a 3-D model of DNA replication.

- What learning styles will be addressed through the assignments in your classes this term?

- Which assignments do you think will be the most challenging for you to complete?

- Which assignments are the most intriguing? Why?

Meeting
expectations

The college will expect that I . . .	To meet that expectation, I will . . .
Example: . . . *learn the material that's presented to me and earn good grades in the process.*	Example: . . . *find ways to translate material from my course work into my learning style preference.*
_____	_____
_____	_____
_____	_____

personality test asks you how outgoing or extroverted you are in certain situations or how reserved or introverted you are in social settings. These questions indicate whether you are Extroverted (E) or Introverted (I). Both left-brain/right-brain inventories, or samples of the complete inventories, as well as the MBTI® can be found in books or online sources.

Other inventories, such as the Dunn and Dunn Learning Styles Assessment and the PEPS Learning Styles Inventory, focus not only on how a person prefers to take in information, but also on a person's social and environmental learning preferences. These types of inventories provide a thorough view of how you prefer to learn, including the temperature of the room, the amount of light and sound, or the preference for moving about as you learn.

Regardless of which learning theory leads you to greater personal insight, as stand-alone models they are only partially useful unless you use the information to benefit your situation. The purpose of a learning styles inventory is to provide you with a basic understanding of the factors that affect your learning preferences so that you can use this information to create an individualized and flexible learning plan for the various tasks and assignments that you will experience while you are in college.

Ultimately, greater personal understanding and self-knowledge leads to action, and this learning styles inventory provides you with not only information about how you prefer to learn, but also the road map for the journey to completing tasks and goals successfully.

There are many ways of analyzing yourself and creating a plan of action for your work in college, but no single inventory, assessment, or work plan will completely reflect the exceptional person you are or your unique circumstances. No matter what inventory you take or what you learn about how you prefer to learn, the results are not the final verdict on your abilities and potential.

G R I T
Tenacity

> Gaining insights into yourself is a vital part of your journey. Part of being a gritty learner is taking advantage of every opportunity to learn more and working relentlessly on ways to both leverage your natural tendencies and minimize your weaknesses.

A Learning Style Inventory Can Help You Determine Your Learning Preferences

Knowing your learning style preferences provides a foundation for understanding yourself in other aspects of your life. Information about what you like and dislike, how you relate to others, and how to work productively will help you achieve your goals. The VAK learning styles inventory, which you can take for yourself in the My Student Success Lab (MSSL), will help you identify your particular learning style preferences. Consider the results of the inventory as information about a part of who you are. Your values, dreams, mission statement, goals, and learning style work together to create a more complete picture of who you are and how to get where you want to go.

the unwritten rules
of Learning Preferences

- **Your professors will present information in a way that favors their learning preference.** Don't expect your professor to provide course information or design class activities that accommodate your preference. Instead, you'll need to study materials from the course on your own in a way that helps you the most.

- **Emerging technologies are making it easier to accommodate your learning style preferences.** The growing popularity of educational content in video form, such as the instructional videos from the Khan Academy (www.khanacademy.org), can help learners who favor audio and visual information more than written text. Also helpful is the presentation tool called Prezi, which is emerging as an alternative to PowerPoint. The growing use of audio podcasts and iTunesU to accompany class lectures is another example of technology's support of learning style differences.

- **It's best not to define yourself by a single learning preference.** As you take the various inventories and tests that are mentioned in this chapter, don't just look for your dominant learning style preference. Note also what your secondary preferences are. Your success as a learner will require you to draw on a variety of learning preferences, depending on the type of content and the professor's expectations. In fact, if you discover that a visual learning style is your second or third most preferred style, you may want to stretch yourself in college to use visual depictions of concepts whenever possible to develop and refine that style of thinking.

Your Classroom and Study Tactics Can Reflect Your Learning Preferences

Note taking is an essential part of the college experience, whether it is taking notes while listening to a lecture or reading to prepare for class. How you decide to take notes may very well depend on how you prefer to take in information and learn. The following are strategies for those who have visual, auditory, kinesthetic, or a combination of those learning preferences.

VISUAL LEARNERS. Visual learners often prefer to view information when listening to a lecture. Visuals could be presentation slides, videos, or props that are used for demonstration, but if none are used, visual learners may want to create their own visual representations in their notes.

Take, for example, a possible lecture on academic integrity. An instructor may talk through or write down a few key ideas on the board or in handouts that look like this:

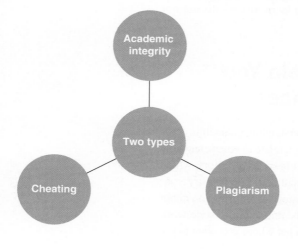

****Academic Integrity—doing what is right academically even in the face of adversity

*Two kinds of violations of academic integrity include cheating and plagiarism.

Plagiarism comes in several varieties, but the two most common are no documentation and cut-and-paste. There are also self-plagiarism, following too close to original, word-for-word, and buying papers . . .

A visual learner may take that information and create a visual representation of the definitions and types like the one at left as a beginning of his or her visual representation.

GRIT GAINER™

GRIT GETS YOU WHAT YOU NEED   Rather than simply accepting what you're given, show some GRIT and go get or create what you need. Professors won't always cater to your preferred learning style or intelligences, but with some real effort you can learn what you need. Ask yourself, "How can I study for or convert this lesson into something that fits my style, so it really sticks?"

AUDITORY LEARNERS. For auditory learners, it may be tempting to listen only rather than write down the essence of what is being said. However, taking notes will be essential to recalling the information later. Recording lectures—with permission from your professor—may benefit auditory learners.

KINESTHETIC LEARNERS. The act of taking notes by writing them or typing them provides kinesthetic learners with a physical activity that makes remembering what has been written easier. Kinesthetic learners can benefit from using physical activity or objects when they review their notes shortly after taking them. For example, if you are using formulas to calculate volume in your math class, you may want to review your notes by creating your own volume problems and solutions with common household items. The act of pouring

© LENETSTAN/SHUTTERSTOCK

Take into account your learning style preference when you are making a study plan.

and measuring water and then calculating your measurements will make it easier to remember the process when you complete homework problems or take a test.

Choose a Study Strategy That Enhances Your Learning Style Preference

Just as note taking with your learning style preference will help you take more meaningful notes, consider using your learning style preference to help you study for your courses. A visual learner, for example, may benefit more from reading through notes and reviewing images that represent the material. These may be from the textbook or presented during lecture, or may be images created by the learner herself when she took notes over the material, such as a mind map.

Mind maps are visual representations of information and their connection with the pieces of information. Although there is a basic structure for a mind map, the creator can customize the visual image with colors and symbols that make the most sense to him. The key to the mind map is to connect the information in meaningful ways to create relationships among the pieces of information. Exhibit 5.1 shows an example of a mind map. Other study strategies for visual learners can include reviewing videos of the concepts or processes that are part of the course.

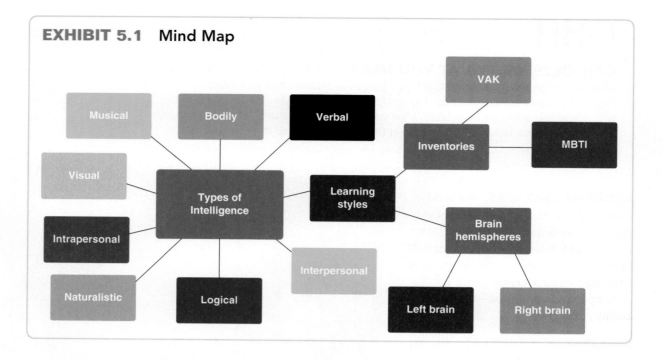

EXHIBIT 5.1 Mind Map

Study strategies for auditory learners can include reading notes aloud or talking through the concepts. An auditory learner can record notes and play them back or participate in a study group and take turns talking through the content and listening. There may also be video or audio files available as part of the course content that could be used to supplement studying.

Kinesthetic learners may want to include practice questions in their studying. For math courses, kinesthetic learners may want to work through practice problems; for any course that requires a short discussion or essay, they may want to practice writing responses and creating outlines for longer essays. A good way for a kinesthetic learner to study for an art history class, for example, is to recreate the artwork she is studying. No need to strive for masterpiece quality when recreating works of art; the physical activity of drawing the wavy lines in the background of Edvard Munch's *The Scream* will help you recall the piece on an exam.

GRIT
Instinct

Being a gritty learner means asking yourself, "What would be the best way to come at this so I learn as much as possible in the most efficient way?" There are countless ways to master the material. Keep trying fresh approaches to find the ones that work best for you.

Your Learning Preferences Can Help You Explore Major and Career Options

Discovering your learning style preference and your personality type can help you set realistic short-term and long-term goals. For example, confirming that you have a visual learning preference and that you are organized and work well with deadlines may help you realize that your long-term goal of being a designer will work well with who you are and how you learn and work. However, identifying your style and type should not limit your choices or keep you from working on areas of your learning style and personality that may be weaker or get less attention.

If you are a strong visual learner, but you are taking a class that relies on listening effectively and critically, you should use that opportunity to become a better listener and improve your aural learning style by following the listening tips that are discussed in another chapter.

Likewise, if you work better alone and have a strong kinesthetic learning style preference, choosing a career as a computer technician may play to your strengths, but you may also find yourself working with others collaboratively and communicating frequently in writing and verbally. See Exhibit 5.2 for examples of careers and majors as they connect to learning style preferences.

One way to see the relationship between learning preferences and career choices is to ask people who are successful in their careers about their own learning preferences. Look for patterns and exceptions. For example, do people who excel in the accounting field tend to favor one style of learning preference over others? How about successful architects? Identifying these patterns can be informative, but shouldn't be discouraging or restrictive for your own decisions. For example, if you favor a kinesthetic learning style, but have a strong interest in a graphic design career, you may discover ways to take advantage of your distinctive style to develop new and creative methods for developing visual depictions of concepts and information.

Whatever your learning style strength and personality preferences are, consider how other styles and types will factor into your short-term and long-term educational goals. Then, look for opportunities to strengthen those less-developed sides of your learning style and personality so that you are more comfortable in a variety of situations and so that you are a well-rounded person.

© BROCREATIVE/SHUTTERSTOCK

Your learning style preference may also influence your career choice.

Resilience

One of the biggest challenges you may face is when you are working on a team project with people with different learning styles and needs. Use your GRIT and ask yourself (or your team), "How can we leverage the upside and minimize the potential downsides of our differences?"

EXHIBIT 5.2 Learning Style Preferences, College Majors, and Careers

Learning Style Preference	College Majors	Careers
Visual	Art, graphic design, architecture, video production	Art teacher, artist, graphic designer, architect, interior designer, video producer
Auditory	Music, communications, counseling	Musician, music educator, marketing director, public relations director, counselor
Kinesthetic	Sciences, sociology, computer technology, culinary arts, theater	Nurse, doctor, therapist, networking specialist, computer technician, actor, director

THE GRIT ADVANTAGE

Learning and GRIT go hand in hand. The more GRIT you show, the more you learn. Be a gritty learner and put this chapter into practice by asking yourself these questions:

1. How can I take full advantage of my natural intelligences and learning style to get the most of this lesson or class?
2. Where can I best apply greater effort and keep trying, so I can overcome some learning challenges I may face?
3. What challenges might I normally avoid that, if I were to take them head-on, might help me learn and grow the most?
4. What's the one tip, idea, or discovery from this chapter that I need to apply immediately to become a more effective learner?

HOW GRITTY ARE YOU?

Now that you've completed this chapter, how committed are you to:

1. Applying these techniques to become a more effective, efficient, and active learner?

   Zero Commitment **0** —————————————————————— **10** Fully Committed

2. Refusing to be defined by any labels and doing what it takes to learn in any situation?

   Zero Commitment **0** —————————————————————— **10** Fully Committed

3. Relentlessly improving how you learn?

   Zero Commitment **0** —————————————————————— **10** Fully Committed

6 Listening and Note Taking

Chapter goals to help you get in, get through, get out, and get paid:

This chapter will help you develop effective listening and note-taking skills so you can get in, get through, get out, and get paid. To graduate, you need to complete all of the courses in your degree plan, and each of these courses will require you to listen well and take informative notes to help you perform well on quizzes, tests, and projects. You will also need to learn how to minimize distractions and work with your peers.

To get a great job, you'll need to listen well and take accurate notes so that you can learn the technical requirements of your job, complete the tasks you've been given, and solve customers' and work teams' problems. You will also need to identify when you need more help and how to access it.

To meet those goals, this chapter will help you:

- Practice methods that help you listen more effectively
- Identify barriers to listening
- Apply different note-taking strategies to each of your classes
- Apply **GRIT** to strengthen your capacity to stick with it and not give up until you get or learn what you need

MyStudentSuccessLab™

Log in to MyStudentSuccessLab.com to deepen your **GRIT** mindset and build the skills you'll need to get through the college experience.

Laura's Story

© MONKEY BUSINESS IMAGES/SHUTTERSTOCK

Laura settled into a seat in the front row of her world civilization class.

"The clip we are about to watch," her professor said, "discusses the ancient library in Timbuktu."

"I would much rather watch these videos than listen to a lecture," a classmate named Jamie whispered, causing Laura to miss her professor's explanation of the video.

"Hey? Do you have an extra pen?" Jamie asked, loud enough to be heard over the video. She handed him a pen and made a note to fill in any gaps she had from being distracted.

After the video, Laura's professor provided the information that she had been waiting on: "You have the material that was assigned for reading, the information I cover in the lecture, and then anything else that I bring in. All of this should be studied for the test," said the professor.

"And she will put everything on the test," thought Laura. Even with help from her mentor and the tutor in the learning assistance center, Laura had her work cut out for her: The book was arranged chronologically, but her professor lectured on causes and effects in history. Then there were the tests that cover major themes, such as important reformers or federal policies. Her notes seemed like a jumbled mess. Laura struggled in this class to find the right note-taking method to accommodate all the different types of information.

As Laura headed out of class, her talkative classmate Jamie stopped her. "Do you want to share notes and study together? I don't have much written down, and I noticed you take good notes," he said.

Laura didn't have much time to think about whether it would be helpful to study with someone who seemed to be so disorganized and inattentive, but she knew she would need help, too.

"Sure. Bring your notes and book and we can meet in the library," she said before heading to her next class.

Now, what do you think?

- What would you do if you missed hearing important information because someone or something was distracting you?
  - **a.** Not worry; I will figure it out on my own
  - **b.** Ask someone else after class what I missed
  - **c.** Panic that I missed something important
  - **d.** Immediately email the professor, concisely explain my concern and strategy, and ask for any advice on how to make sure I've filled any gaps so I can do well on the test

- If you felt you needed extra help improving your listening and note-taking skills, what would you do?
  - **a.** Go to a tutoring lab to get assistance
  - **b.** Talk to a friend who also has difficulty
  - **c.** Just try harder
  - **d.** Ask the advice of a few of the best students I know
  - **e.** Nothing; if I cannot do it on my own, I will just deal with the consequences

Success in Class Begins with Preparation

In college, as in life, preparation is a key to success. Much of your academic success will be determined by the preparation you make for your classes before they even begin. Just as you would invest time and effort to prepare for a first date, a job interview, or a meeting with high-level executives, so should you prepare yourself for class before you walk into the classroom. Because a great deal of information is typically shared during class, effective preparation will be particularly important in helping you to listen well, organize what you hear with effective notes, and remember and recall the information later when you need it for projects, exams, and your career. Here are a number of recommendations that can help you prepare effectively for class.

1. **Read and study preassigned materials.** Your professor will often provide a syllabus that tells you what chapters or other written content is assigned for each day of class. If you take time to read the assigned materials before class, thus making you more familiar with the content that is discussed in class, you will be able to learn more effectively and, in the long run, spend less time preparing for quizzes and exams later in the term. Your professor might even provide a copy of the lecture notes in advance via the course website. If so, print them and bring them to class. When you build your schedule for the term, include time for reading the course materials

Preparing to listen and staying focused will make listening—and remembering what was said—more effective.

before class. If you step into a class and have already read the assigned material, you will better understand what the professor is talking about, you will be familiar with the terminology and concepts, and you will have good questions to ask in class for clarification and further learning. This will help you take notes more effectively and will enhance your class participation effectiveness.

2. **Minimize out-of-class distractions.** There will be times during your college experience when you will have to work late, stay up all night with a sick baby, or help a friend who has just had a crisis. If not handled well, these stressful experiences could affect your performance in class. As much as possible, leave your personal life at the door and concentrate on the class that you are sitting in. How?

   - Put time into your schedule to address personal matters.
   - Turn off your cell phone—don't just set it to vibrate—while in class.
   - Build in 5 to 10 minutes before every class to clear your mind of any personal issues or other distractions to prepare for the class at hand. Reviewing the assigned readings or your notes from last class can aid in this process.

3. **Prepare for class psychologically by preparing physically.** Make sure you have eaten something before each class so that you won't be interrupted by a growling stomach. Moreover, dress in layers in case the room is an uncomfortable temperature. Nothing is more distracting than being too hot or too cold. Getting plenty of sleep the night before class will also help you pay attention and listen effectively. Although adequate sleep may be a luxury if you work a late shift or if you get up in the middle of the night to take care of a child, be sure you make an effort to get a good night's sleep often. You won't be able to maintain high concentration and retention or even good health without adequate rest. Review Exhibit 6.1, which provides tips for preparing to listen.

EXHIBIT 6.1 Tips for Preparing to Listen

Tip	Explanation	Example
Prepare ahead of time.	Read all pages from textbooks, handouts, and extra material that your professor assigns or mentions.	Before the lecture on the American Dream in Arthur Miller's *Death of a Salesman*, read the entire play.
Minimize in-class distractions.	Make sure that you have few, if any, items or people near you that can get your attention.	Turn your phone to silent mode and stow it in your backpack before walking into class.
Maintain a positive attitude.	Stay positive about a class no matter what others have said negatively about it or what you have experienced so far.	On your way to class, think about five positive aspects of the class that will help you achieve your ultimate academic or career goal.
Minimize out-of-class distractions.	Your situation and thoughts can get in the way of concentrating on what is being said. Work to focus on the present, not the past or the future.	If there is something on your mind, write down your concerns before going to class and promise yourself to think about it after class is over.
Prepare physically.	Take care of yourself by getting enough rest and food or drink before you go to class. Wear appropriate clothing so that you will be comfortable.	Grab your jacket, an energy bar, and a bottle of water before you go to your classes.

GRIT
Growth

Effective Listening Is Both Active and Critical

Active listening is a term that you may hear in college classes; someone who listens actively is concentrating on what is being said and taking steps to remember the information.

> To be an active listener, you must decide that listening is a worthwhile activity and that important information will be shared. You have to show some GRIT and commit.

The following tips are intended for those who want to listen actively and effectively.

1. Write down important facts, concepts, and terminology in a notebook designated for that specific course.

2. Use visual tools (charts, tables, arrows, numbers) to organize content in notes.

3. Raise your hand and ask questions to clarify content or resolve confusing concepts.

4. Maintain an upright posture in your chair to keep your body in an alert position.

5. Create acronyms or other mnemonic devices (see Chapter 8) to help organize and remember the information.

6. Write down questions, feelings, opinions, and other reactions in the margins of the notes for later review and consideration.

7. Maintain a positive mindset about the class. Look for connections between content discussed in class, other classes, and your future career. Consider the possibility that at any moment, you could learn something new—this is an exciting perspective that can keep you engaged in the class, no matter what the topic or how it's being discussed.

Meeting
expectations

The college will expect that I . . .	To meet that expectation, I will . . .
Example: . . . *minimize listening barriers while in class.*	Example: . . . *store my phone in my backpack to keep me from being distracted and sit at the front of the classroom.*

8. Avoid in-class distractions.
   - Clear your desk of anything except your textbook, a pen, and paper. Stow other items in your backpack or underneath your desk or table.
   - If you need to get anything out of your backpack during class, such as a dictionary, minimize the disruption by being as quiet as possible.
   - If you find yourself next to a chatty classmate or one who likes to write notes to you, simply move. Even if you are politely listening or reading her messages, you will be guilty of disrupting the class by association. Talkative classmates make it difficult for you and others to listen, and they distract you from taking good notes.

To Listen Critically Is to Listen Well

Active listening, much like active reading, involves focusing on the task at hand and concentrating on what is being conveyed. Another part of listening effectively is listening critically, or processing and evaluating what you have heard.

Listening critically will help you make decisions about what is important and what is not, what is objective and what is subjective. Listening critically is a skill that should be practiced regularly. Getting good at it means you have to persist, sometimes struggle through frustrations. Your college professors will invite you to think critically and will challenge your assumptions at times. This may feel uncomfortable, but critical thinking is a key part of learning. As you get more comfortable with listening actively and critically, you will move from merely listening and taking notes that reflect what your instructors have said to listening to evaluate and ask questions of the notes you have taken. Here are some questions to consider as you work on listening critically:

- **Speaker.** Is the speaker a credible source? How do I know? What possible biases does he or she have? What is his or her experience with the topic?
- **Message.** What is the speaker's purpose? What are the details he or she uses to convey the message?
- **Details.** Is the speaker using facts or opinions? How do I know? Which type of details work best for what the speaker is trying to convey?
- **Self-knowledge.** What do I already know about the topic? How does what the speaker is saying conflict with or support my beliefs and opinions? Do I feel I have learned something new?
- **Larger picture.** How does what the speaker is saying fit into the larger picture? How can I relate the message to something I already know about life or the world at large? Are there any connections between what I have heard and what I have experienced?

It's in the
syllabus

By looking at your syllabus, determine how information will be presented in the course.

- Will it be presented by chapters, topics, or units?
- What are the note-taking expectations for the class?
- Is that information in the syllabus or did you learn it from your professor or other students?

Answering some of these questions will get you started on the right path to listening critically. Even though you are listening critically and mentally asking questions of what you are hearing, you still need to tune in when you hear something that you don't agree with or don't understand.

Remember, too, that "critical" does not mean "negative." If you find that what you are hearing is not holding up to what you know about the subject or the speaker is not credible, you can still ask questions that are respectful and curious. Most speakers do not mind being politely challenged or debated.

Tenacity

Great note takers and listeners don't typically start out that way. Bottom line, you have to want it. You have to invest. And you have to commit. Take on the challenge of focusing intently and taking notes throughout, in spite of how well you do or don't understand whatever's being taught. Stick with it. You'll only get better if you give it your best, most tenacious effort.

Taking Notes Is Part of the Listening Process

There are numerous methods of taking notes for a class. Your goal should be to find the note-taking strategy that works best for you. Remember that you may have to adapt your note-taking style to each course, each teaching style, and each of your learning style strengths. For example, outlining may work well in a history course in which the instructor writes key terms on the board and organizes her lecture around these key ideas. If your professor prefers unstructured discussion, you will need to adapt your note-taking strategy to make the most of disorganized information.

Whatever you choose for the particular course, your learning style, and the specific situation, there are a few tips that you need to remember when taking notes.

- Listen for the main ideas. Instructors will slow down and emphasize information, terms, and definitions. They may even use verbal signposts, such as "The most important thing to remember is . . . ," "This may appear on an exam," or "Two crucial points about . . . ." If the instructor writes or hands out an outline, you can be sure that it contains the main points of the lecture.

- Leave plenty of "white space" (blank space on paper) when taking notes. Don't try to fill your page with as much information as possible. You will need the white space to add more notes or to synthesize ideas once you have reviewed.

- Review your notes as soon as possible after class. Waiting two weeks to review your notes will ensure that you won't remember everything that you have written or how it all fits together. Most experts suggest that you review your notes within two days of the class.

Knowing How Information Is Presented Can Improve Your Note Taking

Instinct

Learning to listen effectively is the first step to taking good notes, but you will also benefit from understanding how information can be presented during a lecture.

As you attend more classes, you will probably notice that professors have a certain way in which they present their material. Some will follow the textbook. Others will lecture only on new material that cannot be found in the textbook or other course materials. Others will present a combination of the two methods. Reading assigned chapters and materials before you attend class will allow you to determine which information in the lecture is new and which has been covered in assigned reading materials.

Here are some of the different ways that course material might be presented organized:

1. Chronological: Details arranged in time (first this happened, then this happened, etc.)

Example of Chronological Lecture Notes

1801: United Kingdom of Great Britain is created

Play spy. Focus in and try to decode not just what's being taught, but *how*.

1803: Louisiana Purchase is made by Thomas Jefferson

1815: Battle of Waterloo signals end of Napoleon's career

2. Cause/effect: Details arranged by presenting a cause and then its effects or an effect and its causes

   Example of Cause/Effect Lecture Notes

   Cause: Civil War

   Effects: Slavery ended, industrialism began, the nation was brought back together, the federal government proved stronger than the states

3. Compare/contrast: Details arranged by similarities and differences

   Example of Compare/Contrast Lecture Notes

   Similarities between Robert Frost and Walt Whitman: They were males; they used nature in their poetry; and they were considered "poets of the people."

   Differences between Frost and Whitman: Frost's poetry is more structured, whereas Whitman's is open and loose; Whitman's speakers are more positive and upbeat than Frost's; Whitman lived during the 19th century whereas Frost lived in both the 19th and 20th centuries.

4. Most important/least important: Details arranged in order of importance; the most important detail can come first with minor supporting details to follow, or the least important details can start a list that works to a major detail

   Example of Most Important/Least Important Lecture Notes

   Self-awareness (purpose of education)

   Values

   Goals

   Mission

   Personality type

   Learning style

GRIT
Instinct

Part of being a gritty learner is adjusting your approach or strategy to make sure you get what you need, no matter what.

the unwritten rules
about Listening and Note Taking

- **The ability to listen well is arguably more critical to your success than your ability to speak well.** Why else would you have two ears, but only one mouth?

- **By preparing for class, listening well, and taking good notes, you can actually reduce your study time.** Professors will be hesitant to suggest this, because they don't want anyone to reduce how much time they devote to studying, but the fact is that if you listen to, process, and organize information effectively the first time, it doesn't take as long to review and remember the information the second time.

- **Sitting next to your friends or other students you know in class might not be the best idea.** The probability of distracting activities and conversations increases when you are in close proximity to people you know. It might be socially awkward to tell your friend that you're not going to sit next to her in class, but your academic performance stands to gain from making wise choices.

© WAVEBREAKMEDIAMICRO/SHUTTERSTOCK

■ Taking good notes is an important part of the learning process.

Once you understand how your professor tends to present information, or how the information is structured in the course materials, you can develop your own strategy for organizing your notes. Here are some alternative strategies that you can try for yourself.

OUTLINING. Using an outline is a good method for taking notes if the instructor is organized and offers information in a logical pattern. Some instructors encourage outlining by writing key words and concepts on the board or an overhead projector. If your instructor organizes lectures or class discussions in this manner, you will be able to write an outline for your notes quite easily. The key to making your outlines effective will be to provide plenty of space between the items so that you can fill in the blank spaces with extra information.

THE CORNELL SYSTEM. Cornell University professor Dr. Walter Pauk (2004) developed a system for note taking that has been popular with many students. The Cornell System, also known as the T-System, is ideal for those who benefit from the visual impact of organized notes.

The key to the Cornell System is dividing your notebook paper before you begin writing. To do so, draw a horizontal line across your piece of paper two inches from the bottom of the page and a vertical line from the horizontal line to the top of the page about two inches from the left margin. The page should look like Exhibit 6.2.

The largest area, the right column, is used for taking notes during class. The left column is used for writing down questions as you take notes, such as material you don't understand during the lecture or possible exam questions that you think about as you are writing. At the bottom, the final section is reserved for summarizing your notes as you review them. The act of summarizing should help you understand and remember the information.

Adapting Your Notes for Each Discipline

ART. In an art appreciation class, you will need to identify eras (20th century), movements (Cubism), and artists (Picasso), as well as the characteristics seen in drawings, paintings, and sculpture. Quickly sketching the works in your notes and listing the characteristic details will help you record the information you are receiving through lectures. You may also notice that in the study of art there are times of intense change (usually coinciding with a world or cultural event) followed by artists who imitate or slightly modify the new style. As you review your notes, look for patterns and points of contrast within groups of artwork.

MUSIC. The same suggestions for an art appreciation class will work when you take notes in a music appreciation class. Instead of recreating a painting or sculpture in your notes, you may need to write down descriptions of what you are hearing and what the sounds remind you of. Are the sounds fast or slow? Do you hear one instrument or many? Does it sound like a stampede or a trip down a lazy river? "Translating" music samples into written notes, as well as reviewing music clips on your own, will strengthen your understanding of the material. As with your art notes, upon review, look for patterns across

---

EXHIBIT 6.2 Cornell System

Add questions or important notes here.	Write notes here.

Add summary of notes here after you read through them.

movements and eras and denote contrasting ideas and elements. Don't be discouraged if the first few attempts are frustrating, or if you have to struggle to get good at this skill. Once you do, it will make learning that much easier.

LITERATURE. Taking notes in a literature class will require that you have completed the assigned readings before class and that you have annotated and highlighted your text. Because literature classes, even survey classes, focus more on discussion than on lecture, you will want to be prepared to take notes on the analysis. As with music and art classes, being familiar with basic terminology before you get to class will help you take better notes. Challenge yourself to learn and even use any new terms as they pop up. As you review your notes, look for ideas that pull the different readings together.

LANGUAGES. Foreign language classes center more on speaking and interacting than on listening to a lecture. Taking notes will not necessarily be advantageous—you will need to focus all your attention on listening actively, processing what is heard, and interacting. Daily preparation is essential to learning foreign languages; take notes as you encounter new material and ask questions in class to get clarification on anything you do not understand. Any notes you do take should be reviewed soon after the class. As you review your notes, categorize material, such as "irregular verbs," and include any tips for using or remembering the parts of language.

SCIENCE. Concepts and processes are key in science classes and your notes will reflect that. Prepare for class by reading assigned material, making note of new vocabulary words, and studying diagrams and figures in the text and handouts. As you review your notes, consider the different ways that you can represent these concepts and processes visually and physically to help you remember them better.

HISTORY. History class lectures are usually presented in chronological order, so using the previous tips for information that follows a time sequence will help you take notes in this class. However, you will also be required to move beyond specific dates and events by considering overall themes, ideas, and movements. In addition to chronological order, lectures may also use a cause/effect organization. An example of a lecture topic in a history class is "the economic and social effects of the end of the Civil War." As you review your notes, look for major themes and aim to recall actions that have led to important events.

MATH. Taking good notes in your math classes will require that you prepare and attend each class meeting. As with foreign languages, studying for math should be an everyday occurrence because the skills you learn in each class build on the ones you learned in the class before. When reviewing your notes, you may want to recopy them and make sure that you understand, line by line, each problem that you are copying. If you have any questions, you can write them in the margins of your notes and ask questions during the next class meeting.

By preparing in advance for class, listening both actively and critically, and taking effective notes, you can greatly enhance your college success.

© TOMASZ TROJANOWSKI/SHUTTERSTOCK

■ Your note-taking strategy may differ depending on the course you are taking.

GRIT
Resilience

As with any class, you can be more resilient and reduce your frustrations when you ask questions, especially if you are having trouble following the steps of a process. Gritty students get the answers they need to proceed. Exercise your GRIT to work through and get past barriers. Taking on, navigating, even busting through barriers is what separates the best from the rest. Each time you do, you will get stronger and better equipped to take on the next one.

GRIT
Tenacity

It takes trial and error to figure out the best approach. Don't give up.

THE GRIT ADVANTAGE

Critical listening and note taking are your power tools. Whether you are trying to land a great job, save a ton of time, enjoy healthy relationships, improve your grades, or simply get more out of your education, these tools make all the difference. Without them, school can be demoralizing. With them, you can rise to your best. It takes work. That's where the GRIT advantage kicks in.

Whenever you face an obstacle, don't blame it, *use* it. Simply ask yourself, "How can I minimize and get past this obstacle as quickly as possible?"

Go after the right stuff in the best ways. Step back, reassess, and clarify what you want and why you want it. Then reroute or adjust how you go after it to make each attempt easier, simpler, and faster.

Now you are ready to relate this to your own life:

- Practice active listening by focusing on what the speaker is saying and remember what she has said before responding or forming an opinion.

- Start listening critically by considering the speaker's authority, credibility, and accuracy.

- Begin to identify listening barriers that you face in your classes and practice strategies for eliminating them.

- Choose the best note-taking strategy for the type of class you are taking.

- Review your notes within a day or two of taking them.

HOW GRITTY ARE YOU?

Now that you've completed this chapter, how committed are you to:

1. Regularly practicing being a better listener?

   Zero Commitment 0 ————————————————————————————— 10 Fully Committed

2. Not blaming others or other things when you have difficulty listening or remembering what you have heard?

   Zero Commitment 0 ————————————————————————————— 10 Fully Committed

3. Employing the best strategies and going after the most important goals?

   Zero Commitment 0 ————————————————————————————— 10 Fully Committed

4. Not getting distracted while listening or taking down notes?

   Zero Commitment 0 ————————————————————————————— 10 Fully Committed

7 Reading and Note Taking

In order to get in, get through, get out, and get paid, you will need to read—a lot—and understand and remember what you read. This skill will be as important after you graduate as it is while you are in college. This chapter will help you develop reading strategies and habits that you can apply immediately.

To meet those goals, *this chapter will help you:*

- Create reading notes using active and critical reading
- Apply your **GRIT** to upgrade your reading skills, with all the rich benefits it provides
- Take good notes while reading
- Combine class and text notes

MyStudentSuccessLab™

Log in to MyStudentSuccessLab.com to deepen your **GRIT** mindset and build the skills you'll need to get through the college experience.

Evan's Story

© MONKEY BUSINESS IMAGES/SHUTTERSTOCK

To Do

- 54 pages of biology textbook
- 72 pages of aviation textbook
- 213 pages of autobiography

Even though he could bench press hundreds of pounds, Evan felt weak when he thought about reading. Evan soon discovered that college without reading was like kickboxing without sore muscles.

When he ran into Michael in the hall after class earlier last week, he complained about what he had to do and why he didn't want to do it.

"Evan, I know exactly what you need to do. I just got help with my algebra homework, and the tutor explained it in a way that I could get it," Michael said.

"It's not that I don't know what to do," Evan said to Michael. "I just don't like to read. It's boring."

Michael laughed. "It does seem boring at first," he said, "but you will get better at reading the more you do it."

"I don't think I want to get that good at it," Evan joked.

Despite his joking, Evan went to the only place he knew can help him: the tutoring center.

Now, what do you think?

- What would you do if you did not want to read an assignment?
  a. I would dig in anyway and wade through it no matter how long it takes
  b. Not do it or reluctantly do it; I cannot make myself read something I am not interested in
  c. Break down the reading assignment into parts and start working on it a little at a time

- What strategies could you use make reading assignments more enjoyable?
  a. Just do it no matter what
  b. Learn how to use different reading strategies to read with less difficulty and more interest
  c. Give up; there are other ways to learn material other than reading about it

Reading Is an Active Process

Reading is important to your college education, career, and personal success because it helps you develop knowledge about a subject; it improves your understanding of others and the world around you; and it helps you understand yourself, which will assist you in making better life choices.

What do you picture in your mind when someone tells you that he or she has been reading for three hours? Perhaps you envision the person reclining in a comfortable chair with a cup of coffee. Although this may be an enjoyable way to read, the reality is that a lot of us would probably fall asleep if we sat in that kind of position for any length of time! When you read books, articles, and online content to learn and study, you'll have a lot more success if you make it a far more active process.

Active reading, a term that you may hear often in college, means that you are fully engaged in reading by focusing your mind and body on the activity. Many first-time students read passively rather than actively and do not fully concentrate on the material. Just reading the words is not enough for college classes. Instead, you must be a part of the process by making sure you comprehend what you are reading.

■ Reading actively includes being focused on what you are reading.

© AREKMALANG/SHUTTERSTOCK

Critical reading is another term that you will hear frequently in college. Some students may think that critical reading means having a negative reaction to what they have read, but it actually involves a series of steps to react and respond to the reading—either positively or negatively, depending on the material. The end goal of critical reading is to question and evaluate the material, not to take it at face value. Critical reading as well as active reading is a set of skills that will take practice to develop. The following sections provide specific strategies for improving both skills.

G R I T
Tenacity

Remember, a big part of GRIT is finding ways to achieve your goals in spite of the frustrations, obstacles, and struggles along the way. Decide to dig deep and do whatever it takes to learn what you need so you get what you want.

Successful Reading Begins with Preparation

The majority of your reading assignments in college will be assigned by your instructors. You will be given handouts, syllabi, and chapters to read in your textbook. How do you manage it all without getting behind and overwhelmed at the start of the semester? Preparation is the key. The following steps will help you successfully prepare for effective reading:

- **Assume all assigned material is important.** When your professors assign content for you to read, it's the result of their careful evaluation of a large volume of material. Take advantage of the fact that they've worked hard to pick the right content for you to read.

- **Organize reading materials according to their length and when they are due.** You will want to begin reading with the most important or urgent assignments first, then work your way through the content.

- **Mark a specific time and place to read on your calendar, preferably at the same time each day.** This will help your mind and body to prepare for the reading task.

- **Find a comfortable, quiet area to read.** This will help you focus on what you are reading.

- **Establish routine breaks from reading.** Get up, walk around the room, get a drink of water, and get the circulation going in your legs again. Taking breaks in which you physically move around the room will help your concentration and keep you from falling asleep.

- **Establish a clear purpose for reading.** For example, if your reading purpose is to understand how food passes through the body's digestive system, then when you sit down with the textbook for your anatomy class, you are in the right frame of mind to absorb this specific information.

- **Take good care of your body and mind throughout the term.** You won't be able to read effectively if you are tired, hungry, or sick. Don't try to force yourself to read if physical or psychological issues distract you. Too much sugar and caffeine and too little sleep can make reading more difficult, as can certain medications and emotional distractions. If you cannot concentrate, return to the material when you are feeling better—but be sure to use this advice sparingly. Sometimes, you will just need to dig and get it done regardless of how you feel.

G R I T
Growth

When it comes to reading, most students focus on quantity over quality. This is a mistake. Instead of putting in longer hours reading more, use the tools in this chapter to read and comprehend better, maybe in less time. It's not how much you read, but *how* you read that matters.

It's in the

syllabus

Review your syllabi and determine how many pages (approximately) you are required to read each week for all of your classes.

- Do some classes require more reading than others? Which ones?
- Are some of the reading assignments harder than others? Which ones?
- How do you plan to handle the reading load this semester?
- Do you expect to keep up with the readings? Why or why not?

Meeting
expectations

The college will expect that I . . .	To meet that expectation, I will . . .
Example: . . . *will read the assigned materials before class.*	Example: . . . *use active and critical reading strategies to study the assigned materials before we discuss them in class.*
_____	_____
_____	_____
_____	_____

Skimming and Scanning Can Be Useful Techniques

Skimming is reading material quickly and superficially, paying particular attention to main ideas. Use this method of reading when you first get a reading assignment because it can help you get a feel for what the material is, how long it is, and how difficult it will be to read. In order to skim a text effectively, you should read the first and last paragraphs, the main headings of each section, and the first and last sentences of each paragraph. Of course, if time is a factor, you can delete some of the steps or add more. Ideally, skimming should be done before in-depth reading. However, sometimes skimming may be the only chance you have to read the material. If this is the case, be sure to pay attention to the major headings of each section and the first and last paragraphs of the material. Don't be surprised, though, if you miss major ideas that are sandwiched in the middle.

Scanning is looking quickly for a specific item or topic as you would scan a website for a particular product or a dictionary for a particular word. Scanning also includes examining the table of contents and index of a book to help you find what you are looking for. Just as with skimming, scanning requires that your eyes move quickly over a page. However, the difference between scanning and skimming is that you know what you want to find and will slow down once you find it. Scanning is particularly useful when reviewing sources to use for a paper. You can determine rather quickly if the source pertains to your topic or not. Once you scan, you can then skim or read the text actively.

Part of scanning a text includes examining its parts. A book consists of several chapters; within each chapter are several sections; within each section are several paragraphs; within each paragraph are a number of sentences; and within each sentence are words and phrases. As you read, look for the connection between the smallest parts of the writing assignment— the words and phrases within sentences—and the biggest parts of the assignment—the entire book or chapter. Also, be sure to review the other information about a reading assignment, such as the title, author, table of contents, chapter titles, introduction, section headings, footnotes, bibliography, and index. As we'll discuss later in this chapter, taking notes while you read and using outlines can help you summarize and organize the various parts of a reading assignment to better understand its purpose and meaning as a whole, as well as individual specific points within it.

Instinct

Because a key element of being a gritty learner is assessing and improving *how* you learn, not just how hard you work to learn, pick the tool that you think would give you the biggest benefit and put it to use immediately, until it becomes hardwired and saves you time.

SQ3R Is a Useful Reading Strategy

In addition to skimming, scanning, and breaking the assigned reading into its composite parts, you might also want to try one of the most popular reading strategies, called SQ3R, which stands for "survey," "question," "read," "recite," and "review."

Tenacity

(S) Survey: Before reading your text closely, start by examining the headings, subheadings, graphics, charts, and references (if included).

(Q) Question: After you look for these major organizational signposts, you can either think about or write down questions that you have. One way to generate questions is to turn headings and subheadings into questions. For example, the subheading "SQ3R Reading Strategy" can be turned into the question "What is the SQ3R reading strategy?"

> Do you know why practice typically fails? Because most people quit. Not you. You know that a huge part of GRIT is trying over and over until you get better. Expect to be weak at a new skill the first time. It only gets more fun from there.

(R1) Read: Read each section, making sure you are concentrating on what you have read.

(R2) Recite: At the end of each section that you have read, say aloud what the section was about and answer the questions that you asked during the Question stage. You may also want to write your answers on note cards to review later.

(R3) Review: Any time after you have completed the first four steps, you will be ready to review what you have read. Some experts suggest reviewing within 24 hours of reading; others recommend reviewing what you have read in short sessions over a period of time.

Active Reading Also Means Critical Reading

While you are actively reading assigned or researched material, you also need to read it critically. In most cases, this will mean rereading the material, especially if it is short. Be sure to allow yourself plenty of time for this activity. At this point in the critical reading process, you do not necessarily need to answer the questions you raise—you will just want to look for places within the material where you want to know more, want clarification, or disagree with the author's conclusion.

Questioning who the author is and his or her purpose in writing the material is the first place to start. Questions to ask include: Is the author an authority? Is he or she credible? Is there an agenda or bias in the writing? If the material comes from a magazine, newspaper, or blog, you will also want to question the purpose of that source. When considering the source, you may ask, "What is the purpose of presenting this material?" If it comes from a newspaper, does the material aim to inform or persuade? Does it present only one side of a debate? If the material comes from a blog or an anonymous website, does the material intend to serve as reliable information, or is it only someone sharing his or her observations with no intention of providing accurate information? Writing these questions in the margins of the text or using a notebook for your questions is a good start to reading critically.

Another important element of information literacy is evaluating what you have read for its usefulness. Just because a book, article, or other content mentions a particular topic that you're studying doesn't mean that it's a relevant source. You need to review the content to determine if it helps you answer the specific questions you have. For example, if you have to write an essay explaining *why* the Congress of the United States includes both the Senate and the House of Representatives, a website that lists all the members of Congress won't be helpful for your assignment. Furthermore, if your assignment requires you to argue in favor of a certain law or legislative act, you need to evaluate the material you read to determine if it provides supporting information.

In the era of Google searches and Wikipedia, it seems easy to find a lot of information about virtually any topic you need to study. The challenge is to evaluate this information for both credibility and relevance. These skills are crucial for your information literacy, and they will serve you well both in college and throughout the rest of your life.

Check your understanding of the differences between active and critical reading by completing Activity 7.1. Place an X in the column to indicate if the statement is part of active or critical reading.

GRIT GAINER™

READ WITH GRIT One way to set yourself apart and increase your chances of successfully getting through, getting out, and getting paid is to become competent or strong at the things others lack. In an era when all of your friends read and exchange micromessages, learning to really read and fully comprehend is a huge advantage.

■ ACTIVITY 7.1 Active versus Critical Reading

Is it active or critical reading?	Active	Critical
Asking if the author is biased		
Looking up words you are unfamiliar with		
Determining the author's main point		
Considering what information the author did not provide		

the unwritten rules
about Reading and Note Taking

- **You cannot multitask while reading material for your classes.** If you have music or the television on while you're reading, or if you're constantly checking your phone or computer for emails, texts, or calls, it will take you at least 30 percent longer to read the material, and you'll remember less of it. Find a quiet place of solitude for reading and you'll have far better results.

- **Experiment with using technology for note taking before committing to it entirely.** Students are increasingly using laptops and tablet computers to take notes during class or reading. Ask your professor before using a laptop or tablet computer in class, and always have a backup pad of paper and pencil or pen for note taking if the technology fails.

- **Your notes from one class will serve you well in future classes.** Be sure to keep your notes throughout your academic career, because you never know when you'll need them. For example, your calculus notes may be very helpful when you encounter a challenge in your statistics or economics class later.

- **Use caution when sharing notes with others.** Talk to your professor about his or her standards of academic integrity as they relate to students sharing notes. Some professors may consider it cheating. Also, keep in mind that your classmate may have overlooked important information or misunderstood a concept when taking notes. If you miss a class, getting notes from someone else is rarely a suitable replacement.

Taking Good Notes Helps You Become a Better Reader

As you have read so far, the act of reading is more than just moving your eyes along a page of words. Instead, reading in college requires that you use a strategy that will help you retain the information and think critically about what you have read. Taking notes as you read, either in your textbook or in a notebook, is an excellent way to remember what you have read and to begin the process of critical reading. Writing down key ideas, terms to look up later, and questions that you have as you read helps you stay focused and improves comprehension.

Writing in the margins of your textbook can be an effective way to take notes, especially if the reading assignment is lengthy. If you don't mind writing directly in your textbook, you can summarize main points that you have read. Writing brief, two- or three-word summaries or questions in the margins will help you make sense of and remember what you have read. Marginal summaries will also help you review the material when you start studying for an exam.

Tenacity

Relentlessly taking notes on everything takes a fraction of the effort and time it takes to try to make it up and learn it all later. GRIT pays off in effort, time, and results!

Annotating in your textbook and writing down critical questions are two methods of further reinforcing what you have read that will help you prepare for listening and note taking in class. Critical questions about the reading might include "How do I know this to be true?" and "What else should be considered?" Annotating your textbook with your own notes will help you not only reinforce main ideas, but will synthesize the information in new ways that will produce connections between concepts, making the material more memorable and more relevant.

If you decide to write in the margins of your textbook, be sure that the book you are writing in is not one that you want to sell back to the bookstore. If you do not want to write in your book but still reap the benefits of summarizing the material, you can write your summaries on a separate sheet of paper or even sticky notes that can be removed at the end of the semester. With either strategy, make sure that you label each piece of paper with the chapter title and page number of the book.

Highlighting in your textbook is another method that students use for taking notes on reading material. A highlighter pen can be used to mark important concepts for review, but be careful that you do not highlight too much information. Over-highlighting the text can have the opposite effect—instead of making it easier to understand key terms and information, too much highlighting can make everything seem of equal importance. If you do use a highlighter pen, use it sparingly. For example, don't highlight more than two sentences in a row. A better method would be to use highlighting and written summaries together for the greatest effect.

Ebooks Are Here!

Electronic books, or ebooks, have been gaining popularity with students, professors, and libraries, and they certainly can be more convenient than printed sources. For example, you may be able to download an ebook on your computer or handheld device and read it without having to go to the library to check it out. Also, some ebooks can cost less than their traditional, printed counterparts. Nonetheless, there are some drawbacks to using ebooks rather than printed books: ebooks are dependent on a student having access to technology, and students cannot sell them back as they can printed texts. You may want to test one out—either using a friend's ebook reader or using an ebook reader at the library—before committing to purchasing an ebook reader to use for a class.

Strategies for reading an ebook are similar to a printed text in that you can preview the overall reading by examining the table of contents and chapter headings, looking for main ideas, and questioning the authority and accuracy of the text. However,

Your reading strategy for ebooks may be different than your reading strategy for print books.

© WAVEBREAKMEDIAMICRO/SHUTTERSTOCK

integrity matters

Reading in college is not optional; rather, it is crucial to success. When you make the commitment to enroll in college, you must follow through by tackling the reading that is part of the experience. You will also need to demonstrate integrity when you do not read—be honest with your instructor, if asked, and be honest with yourself that your progress (or lack of) is related to how well you are preparing for class through active and critical reading.

YOUR TURN

In approximately 250 words, describe a time in which you were confused in class because you did not prepare by reading the assignment beforehand. What was the experience like? What did you learn from the experience?

ebooks have additional tools that can make reading actively and critically easier. Some ebooks allow you to search for certain terms and will highlight them in the text. This can be useful if you are trying to find a specific section in the text. Ebook tools may also include highlighters and notes that you can use to mark important information and record your own ideas. Often, these can be saved while you have access to the ebook. A print function may also be included in some ebooks—although printing the entire book may not be possible, it should allow you to print pages that you need.

Combining Your Class and Text Notes Will Give You the Whole Picture

One of the challenges you'll encounter as you accumulate notes is that you'll have notes from your textbook and other written course materials as well as the notes you've taken during class discussions and lectures. Here are some suggestions for how to integrate all of your notes into a single collection of useful information:

■ Make time to combine your class notes with your reading notes.

© COREPICS/SHUTTERSTOCK

- Develop an outline for your content. Your notes from class and your readings can be integrated by organizing them both into a similar outline based on the key topics or learning objectives that they cover. Start with the main headings from your textbook as a possible outline structure, and compare those headings to the organization and structure of your class notes. You may need to add, remove, or modify some of the headings to accommodate your notes from both sources. Once you have an outline, you can take your class notes and reading notes and place them in the same locations based on their content.

- Rewrite, photocopy, cut, and paste, as desired. Once you have an outline structure for your content, you have several options for getting all the content in the right location.

- You can rewrite your notes into the new outline structure you created—this is helpful because in the process of rewriting your notes you are consciously reviewing them and gaining greater retention of the content in your long-term memory. The downside is that rewriting your notes can take a lot of time.

- If you typed your notes on the computer, you can use the "copy" and "paste" functions in your word processing software program to move content from one location to another. The benefit of this option is that it's fast and relatively easy. The downside is that it requires you to type your notes in the first place, and you're not reviewing the information as much as you would if you were rewriting them by hand.

- If you hand-wrote your notes, you can photocopy them, then use scissors and tape to cut out various sections of content and reorganize them around the outline structure that you created. The benefit of this approach is that it's faster than rewriting all of your notes. The downside is that the process of cutting and taping the content from one piece of paper to another can still be time-consuming.

Whichever method you use, the goal of integrating your reading and class notes is to maximize how much you learn about a concept by drawing information from multiple sources. Also, by comparing the content that your professor discussed in class with what you read, you will be able to identify certain topics that the professor considers most important. Another benefit of integrating your notes from both the readings and class is that you will have a more useful collection of notes from the class to use in subsequent courses. Many of the courses you take during your freshmen year are considered prerequisites, which means that you'll use information and skills from an earlier class to help you in a future class. Keeping good notes will help you refresh your memory in later terms when the concepts reemerge. For example, if you take a precalculus class your first semester, you may need your notes from that class during later semesters when you are taking calculus.

The process of note taking while reading is an important skill, both for your college success and your career success. Regardless of the kind of career that you intend to pursue, the ability to take effective notes while reading will serve you well because so much information is communicated using the written word.

GRIT GAINER™

GOING BEYOND WITH GRIT   One reason GRIT gives you a huge advantage is because gritty students go above and beyond. They do the things other students know they should do, but never bother to do—like combining notes! Ask yourself, "When will I commit one hour of my time (now) to save several hours of frustration (later)?"

THE G R I T ADVANTAGE

Engage your GRIT to get great results by taking on this challenge:

1. Pick the reading assignment you dread the most.
2. Answer this question: If the person who knows you best in the whole world were coaching you on taking notes,
   a) specifically what tool(s) would that person suggest you use, b) how would he or she recommend you do it, and
   c) in what setting (place, time, etc.) would that person recommend you do it to give you the best chance of success?

Apply your own wisdom to every assignment and use your GRIT to keep trying until you prove to yourself it works.

HOW GRITTY ARE YOU?

Now that you've completed this chapter, how committed are you to:

1. Enduring discomfort and frustration to learn better ways to read and take notes?

   Zero Commitment 0 ——————————————————————— 10 Fully Committed

2. Applying at least one new tool to read better and faster within the next 24 hours?

   Zero Commitment 0 ——————————————————————— 10 Fully Committed

3. Being willing to do whatever it takes to become a stronger reader?

   Zero Commitment 0 ——————————————————————— 10 Fully Committed

8 Studying and Test Taking

Chapter goals to help you get in, get through, get out, and get paid:

In order to get in, get through, get out, and get paid, you'll need to perform well on tests. Effective test taking is important not only in college, but even in your career, because many of today's technical fields require testing throughout your career. Even if you battle test-taking anxiety or have struggled with tests in the past, you can overcome those challenges and succeed.

To meet those goals, this chapter will help you:

- Develop effective study habits
- Practice various memory strategies for studying
- Prepare strategies for taking different types of tests
- Demonstrate the **GRIT** it takes to do well studying and performing on tests

MyStudentSuccessLab™

Log in to MyStudentSuccessLab.com to deepen your **GRIT** mindset and build the skills you'll need to get through the college experience.

Four Student Stories: Studying

BOTTOM RIGHT: © ANDRESR/SHUTTERSTOCK
ALL OTHERS: © MONKEY BUSINESS IMAGES/
SHUTTERSTOCK

Studying for their Biology 101 class was becoming an exercise in their own survival. Juanita, Evan, Michael, and Laura formed a study group early in the semester.

"So much work for just one class," Michael said. "It's insane."

Juanita replied, "I'm taking world literature and psychology. The reading alone takes me hours each night."

Michael thought he had studied too much of the wrong things, and Juanita had severe test anxiety.

"Are you starting without me?" Laura asked as she dropped her heavy backpack on the booth seat by Michael.

"Of course not," Juanita said. "Michael was just complaining about how much work this class is."

"My mother finished her degree right before I started school. If she can do it, I think I can," Laura said.

"Does anyone know what the test will cover?" Michael said.

"I have to study everything, even if I don't think it will be on the test," said Juanita. "I suggest we start going over everything that we have done since the first chapter."

Evan offered his advice. "If we just review our notes, we should be fine. When was the last time you failed a test?"

"Because we all seem to have different approaches, it sounds like we would be better off studying by ourselves," said Laura.

Now, what do you think?

- What would you do if your study group had divergent ideas as to how to study best?
  a. Convince them to spend time studying in different ways to accommodate each person's preferences
  b. Study by myself to avoid the distractions of others' needs
  c. Choose the two most effective ways to study and focus on those for the entire group

- How would you prepare for taking a test that will be a challenge for you?
  a. Use my strengths to learn the material in a way that suits me best
  b. Ask the professor what strategies work the best for the material and the type of test
  c. Not change a thing; I already have good study habits

Studying Is a Necessary Lifelong Habit

There is strong evidence that the amount of time students spend practicing what they are trying to learn, or "time on task," is the single greatest predictor of academic success. With this in mind, the best advice is plain and simple—study for all tests; no exceptions. By studying for every test in every class, you're developing the habits needed for success in school, your career, and life.

Here are some specific steps you can take to develop effective study habits:

- **Space out your studying over time.** Put regular, ongoing "appointments" on your calendar specifically for studying the content from each of your classes, and start these appointments the first week of the term. Research has shown that studying in smaller increments of time, such as 30 minutes to an hour, over a longer period of time, such as a week, is more effective than cramming four hours straight the night before.

■ Learning to study with a group is an important strategy for succeeding.

© KONSTANTIN CHAGIN/SHUTTERSTOCK

- **Alternate your study spaces.** Conventional wisdom has advised that always studying in the same familiar place is best, but newer research suggests that varying your environment while studying improves your ability to recall information.

- **Make arrangements for your kids (if applicable).** Make the most of their nap and sleep times, or find a reliable babysitter. If you have classmates who face similar challenges, consider some babysitting swaps to give each of you time to study regularly.

Meeting expectations

The college will expect that I . . .	To meet that expectation, I will . . .
Example: . . . spend considerable amount of time studying for tests.	*Example:* . . . work with a study group to prepare for tests.
_____	_____
_____	_____
_____	_____

- **Set goals for your studying.** Are you trying to memorize content, understand how a process works, or solve a math problem? Take time to know what you're trying to accomplish during each study session.

- **Study actively and practice "retrieval."** Rereading texts and notes is actually *not* a good strategy for learning. New research on learning and memory has shown that actively interacting with the material and practicing "retrieving" the information from memory—as opposed to storing it as one would do when reading passively—is best. The following are strategies for improving your ability to access the information for a test:

  - Rewriting or summarizing your notes in your own words
  - Rearranging the order of the material from most important to least important detail, from least important to most important, or in chronological order
  - Making connections between what you have learned in one chapter, unit, or class and material you have learned in other places
  - Making connections between what you have learned in class and what you have experienced in the real world
  - Explaining concepts to someone else who is not familiar with the topic
  - Making visual representations of the material

GRIT
Instinct

GRIT is about digging deep and doing what it takes to make it happen, even if you have to sacrifice, struggle, and suffer. Instinct is about going at it the best way. So do yourself a favor: decide now or on the first day of the new term what you are going to give up and do without in order to study and achieve your goals. It will save you time and heartache later.

Memory Strategies Can Help You Remember and Learn More Deeply

The good news that we've learned from brain research is that spending more time actively learning a subject can translate into deeper learning, and a gritty mindset toward challenging learning environments will enable you to learn more. Why? Because as you spend more time studying and engaged in active learning with a gritty mindset, you will remember more of what you have learned because you have moved it from your short-term memory to your long-term memory.

When you meet someone for the first time, you will keep that person's name and face in your short-term memory. In general, you can only store five to nine items in your short-term memory. If you try to put too many items in there, you will find that some of them slip away. Try glancing at the following list for 30 seconds. Then, cover up the list and write down the words you remember; the words do not have to be in the order that you see them.

cup	paper	pencil	magnet	ruler	scissors
spoon	towel	tape	apple	knife	straw

Growth

Stop doing what doesn't work and grow your skills. Sure, memorizing takes some work. But, exercise some smart GRIT by using the new, effective ways to memorize more in less time offered in this chapter.

How well did you do? If you remembered five to nine items, then you can consider your memory average. It takes some work, though, to transfer information from your short-term memory to your long-term memory.

Modern technologies like computers, smartphones, and ebook readers make it easy for us to have a lot of information at our fingertips. With information so accessible, we might think that it's no longer necessary to memorize anything anymore. The truth is, however, that effective memorization skills are very important to be a successful college student. Quizzes, tests, and other types of examinations are often "closed book," meaning that you can't have your textbook or other materials available during the test. And because most exams and tests are timed, you wouldn't have enough time to search for information in a book to answer a question, anyway—you either remember the information or you don't. For these reasons, it's very important to develop effective memorization skills.

Mnemonic Devices Can Help You Remember

Mnemonic devices are memory aids or strategies that help you remember items, concepts, or a series of events. Usually, mnemonic devices are not used for deep learning, but there will be times during college when, for example, remembering the names of all the bones in the body or all the constitutional amendments must be conquered before deeper learning can happen. Thus, you may find yourself using mnemonic devices as part of your learning process.

© FOTOINFOT/FOTOLIA

■ Deep learning is improved when you can see how parts of information create a whole picture.

DEVICE 1: THE ROMAN ROOM. Let's go back to the previous list and figure out how you could remember all of the items. Ancient Romans are credited with being able to remember significant amounts of information by using the Roman Room, sometimes called the memory palace or loci method (Foer, 2011). This visualization technique can be useful when trying to remember a string of seemingly unrelated items or complex material that needs to be pulled together.

To create a Roman Room, visualize a familiar place, such as a room in your house. If your room is connected to other rooms, then you will have more "places" to put ideas. When you visualize your room, pay particular attention to the items that are already in the room, such as furniture or favorite pictures, and unique details, such as peeling paint. The more vivid the visualization, the better able you will be to remember the items you place there.

To see the Roman Room or loci method in action, take another look at the list.

cup	paper	pencil	magnet	ruler	scissors
spoon	towel	tape	apple	knife	straw

Can you place these items in your kitchen? Put the straw in the cup and place it in the cabinet. Tape the paper on the front of the cabinet. Place the towel on the counter next to the apple, spoon, and knife. Then, put the pencil, ruler, magnet, and scissors in the drawer.

Take 30 seconds to review this room or visualize your own Roman Room with the items listed. Then, cover up both the list and the description of the room and see how many items you can remember. Write the words on a separate piece of paper.

Did you remember more words this time? If not, then visualization strategies may not be the only type of mnemonic device you need to help you remember lots of information. There are other mnemonic strategies that may benefit different learning style preferences. Acrostic sentences and acronyms are two methods that may help students with a read/write learning style preference.

DEVICE 2: ACRONYMS AND ACROSTIC SENTENCES. Take the first letter of items in a series to form sentences that help you remember the items and their order—forming acrostic sentences. For example, music students remember the order of the treble clef staff, E, G, B, D, F, with the sentence "Every Good Boy Does Fine." To recall the order of biological groupings used in taxonomy, just remember "Kids Prefer Cheese Over Fried Green Spinach" (Kingdom, Phylum, Class, Order, Family, Genus, Species).

Take the first letter of items in a series and spell another word to create acronyms. Here are a few examples of acronyms that we use every day: AIDS (acquired immune deficiency syndrome), SADD (Students Against Drunk Driving), REM (rapid eye movement), and SCUBA (self-contained underwater breathing apparatus). Acronyms have been used to help many students remember terms and the order of items, such as ROY G BIV (to remember the order of the colors in the rainbow—red, orange, yellow, green, blue, indigo, and violet) and FACE (to remember the order of notes in the spaces of the treble staff).

Although there are too many words in the previous list to create an acronym, you can create an acrostic sentence (or two) with the initial letter of each word. Because the order of the items is not important, feel free to rearrange the letters to make your sentence(s).

| C | P | P | M | R | S | (Example: Creative people produce many real skits.) |
| S | T | T | A | K | S | |

DEVICE 3: RHYMES AND SONGS. Though a little more difficult to compose than acronyms and acrostics, rhymes and songs, which often appeal to aural learners, are another type of mnemonic device. Who doesn't remember, "Thirty days hath September . . . " and "In 1492, Columbus sailed the ocean blue"? Again, simple information works best for these memory strategies. It will take more work to remember the economic effects of Columbus' discovery of the New World, for example.

When you have the time to explore the variety of memory strategies, try them out until you find the one that works best for the subject matter and your learning style. However, many students who need a memory strategy need it to work quickly as they are cramming before a test. Those students may be successful in remembering it when they get to the test the next day, but the possibility of their remembering it weeks, months, or even a year later is slim. That is why professors and tutors discourage cramming—it may work some of the time, and it is better than not studying at all for a test, but it often produces more anxiety and stress, and the material is less likely to be in your long-term memory when you need it later.

DEVICE 4: CHUNKING. With that warning, there will be times, nonetheless, when despite your best intentions, you will need a fail-safe memory technique to help you remember key concepts in a short period of time. One method, called *chunking,* is similar to the Roman Room or loci method in that items are grouped together to allow the brain to make connections with the items, making it easier to recall the information later.

To see chunking in action, consider the following 10-digit number:

5114796210

It may be easier to chunk the numbers the way a phone number is divided:

511–479–6210

GRIT GAINER™

A GRITTY MEMORY TAKES PRACTICE Chances are you didn't crawl to school today. Yet you fell countless times when you first tried to stand. Why did you persevere? Because you knew it would pay off. Life is better walking than crawling. Same deal applies to memory devices. It's hard. Show some GRIT and keep going. Your memory will be off walking and running soon.

You probably don't realize that you chunk any time you memorize a phone number or Social Security number. In other words, you are taking the seemingly random numbers and putting them together in groups. The goal in chunking is to reduce a large number of items into only five to nine items. To practice this mnemonic technique, use the following list of key terms: acrostic, acronym, chunking, cramming, loci method, long-term memory, mnemonic device, rhyme, Roman Room, short-term memory.

First, make sure that you know the definitions of each term. Record your definition of the terms listed below:

Acrostic	Acronym	Chunking
Cramming	Loci method	Long-term memory
Mnemonic device	Rhyme	Roman Room
Short-term memory		

the unwritten rules
for Studying and Taking Tests

- **Cramming for an exam or pulling an all-nighter is rarely useful.** If you try to study for an exam only a day or a few hours in advance, you won't remember much of what you study, and the stress caused by your procrastination will probably deplete your creative thinking.

- **Credit is credit, even if it's partial credit.** Let's say you have an essay question on an exam that's worth 20 points, and you're confident that you know part of the answer but not all of it. Take the time to provide the part you do know so you can get some points for the answer.

- **Prepare yourself for the testing conditions as much as the test itself.** Depending on your university's exam schedule, your final exams may take as long as three hours to complete. When's the last time you actually sat in one place for three hours working on a test or exam? You can't prepare for a marathon by running 100-yard sprints. The only way to perform well during a three-hour exam is to

prepare yourself for thinking and writing for that block of time.

- **If you don't understand a question when the professor hands out the exam, privately ask her for clarification.** It will be up to the professor to decide how much help and clarification to provide, but it never hurts to ask. Don't start writing your answer until you completely understand the question.

- **Really long answers are rarely really good answers.** When faced with an essay question about a broad topic, students are tempted to write everything they know about that topic in the hope that something they write will satisfy the professor. We call this the "everything but the kitchen sink" essay answer. This rarely works. Pay attention to the verbs that the professor uses in the question—*compare* is different from *evaluate*—and write an answer that directly answers the question in a complete but concise manner.

Next, group the items together logically. Then, complete the chunking with the remaining terms.

For example, one way to group some of the terms could be:

Mnemonic devices are strategies for remembering items and they include **acrostics, acronyms, rhymes,** and **Roman Rooms.**

How else could the terms be grouped together? Use a separate sheet of paper to group them.

Different Tests and Test Questions Require Different Strategies

Although the terms are usually used interchangeably, a *test* is defined as a set of questions that are used to evaluate one's skills, aptitudes, and abilities on certain topics. Usually, tests assess your knowledge and abilities on a part of a course. An *exam,* however, by definition is an assessment of the material of an entire course. Final exams are sometimes called *comprehensive* or *cumulative exams,* which indicate that they will cover what you have studied all semester or term.

Unless your professor tells you directly what will be on the test, assume that anything that was assigned or covered in class may be there. Just about every college student has a story about taking a test that covered reading assignments and not what was discussed in class. These students were surprised to realize that studying the lecture notes was not enough. The following is a list of items that you may be tested on for any class:

- Material from the lecture, discussion, and in-class and out-of-class activities
- Information provided by a guest speaker
- Information from a workshop or field trip
- Multimedia productions, such as video or audio
- Assigned readings, including chapters in the textbook
- Handouts, including PowerPoint slides and outlines

You can be assured that you will encounter a variety of test types. Take clues from what you do in class to help determine what kind of test questions you may encounter. For example, if your professor spends time applying information from a chapter during class or as an assignment, then you will likely have test questions that will ask you to apply the information as well. Listen for clues that the professor gives you, such as "You should write this down," and "This is a really important point." Other cue phrases include "You may see this again on a test," and "If you saw this on a test, how would you answer it?" When you hear these phrases, write them down and review them when studying over your other notes. A professor who says these things is begging you to take notice!

Test Questions Will Vary, and So Should Your Answers

There are two categories of question types: objective and subjective. Objective questions, which require lower-level thinking because they ask you to recall facts and concepts, usually appear in the form of

It's in the syllabus

Look at your syllabus to get clues about the tests you will have.

- What types of test questions do you anticipate from your classes?
- What evidence in the syllabus leads you to believe you will have certain types of test questions? (Hint: Look at the course description, if included.)
- How often will you have tests?

Tenacity

It's GRIT that will help you get better and better at all kinds of tests. One of the best ways to study is to practice. Get or make up sample test questions. Use a classmate. Test each other. Train your mind by saying after each question, "Again!" Do it over, and over, and over. You will master different formats until you are undaunted by the test.

multiple choice, true/false, fill-in-the-blank, and short answer. Subjective questions ask for your opinion about the material or ask you to apply the material in a new way. Essay and problem solving (critical thinking) questions are labeled subjective because there are a variety of ways the questions can be answered correctly.

Sometimes objective questions are easier to answer because they provide a correct answer within the choices. However, objective questions can demand significant brainpower, especially when you must recall an answer with very few clues, which is often the case with fill-in-the-blank questions. Because objective questions usually have only one correct answer, some students believe that there are no "wrong" answers for subjective questions. That may be true, but there are better ways to answer them. In the following sections we discuss typical test questions and how to answer them.

MULTIPLE CHOICE. When answering multiple-choice questions, the first step is to read the question or statement carefully. Then, mark any special words in the question or statement, such as *not, always,* and *only.* Read each choice carefully and eliminate any answer that is obviously wrong. If you have to guess, eliminate any answer that is misspelled (usually a sign that the instructor has hurriedly added false answers) and any answer that is shorter than the others. Also, pay attention to choices labeled "All of the above" and "None of the above." If you can determine that at least two of the choices are correct, then "All of the above" is probably the correct answer.

When studying for a test that will include multiple-choice questions, be sure you know all of the material well. Practice answering multiple-choice questions by using those in your text (or on a companion textbook website, if one is available), or create your own multiple-choice questions based on the material you are studying. You can work through them yourself as part of your studying or you may share with a classmate who has also created multiple-choice questions and take turns answering them.

Learning to use strategies for different types of test questions can help you eliminate obviously wrong answers.

© FREDERICK BASS/SHUTTERSTOCK

MATCHING. A matching section on an exam presents you with two columns: a list of words or phrases that are to be matched with a list of descriptors. Professors who use matching sections usually require basic recall of information, but you will need to read the directions carefully. There may be more than one match for an item in the list or there may be extra descriptors that are not matched to anything. All of these distracters are there to make sure you know the content well enough to make the right decisions.

First, read through the entire list and choices to match before beginning. Then, determine if there could be multiple matches to a word in the list. Make sure that you have chosen the correct letter to match with each word in the list. If there are a few terms that you don't know for sure, try to use the process of elimination to narrow the possible choices down by matching the terms you do know for sure. Also, because not all terms will be the same type, you may be able to eliminate some descriptors because they do not logically "go with" them.

To study for matching, you will need to know major terms, people, and events from the material. Because professors often use similar definitions and descriptions, rather than those directly from the text or glossary, it may be helpful to rewrite your definitions and descriptions in your own words. If you have a study partner or group, ask them to do the same and share the answers they record.

TRUE/FALSE. True/false questions can be tough even though there are only two possible answers. Guessing or randomly answering true/false questions should be done as a last resort.

integrity matters

Nearly 75 percent of college students admit to cheating at least once (Center for Academic Integrity, 2011). The reasons for cheating are many: Some don't believe that their professors notice or care about their work; others believe that getting the good grade is the most important goal if scholarships and program admissions (such as nursing school) demand high standards. Colleges do take cheating seriously and often have no tolerance for those who cheat. Penalties can range from an F in the course to expulsion from the college.

YOUR TURN

In 250 words, describe why you think such a high percentage of college students have reported cheating. Also, describe what colleges can do to help maintain an environment of academic integrity.

It is better to read the statements carefully, noting key words that could point to the correct answer, such as *frequently, sometimes,* and *a few.* These words usually indicate a true statement. Words such as *never, only,* and *always* usually indicate a false statement. If you're struggling with a particular true/false statement, take a moment to "flip" the statement and see if your answer would switch from true to false or false to true. This can help you work through any double negatives and other somewhat confusing phrases.

Studying for true/false test questions is similar to the study tips described earlier for multiple-choice and matching questions: know the material or course content well enough that when presented with questions about it, you can recognize major concepts and questions. Also, write out sample true/false questions that you think would make good additions to the test. Share with a study partner or group and take turns answering each other's sample questions.

FILL-IN-THE-BLANK/SHORT ANSWER. Fill-in-the-blank and short answer questions require that you recall definitions of key terms or items in a series. To complete these types of questions, first read the sentence or question carefully. Often, points will be lost if you don't answer exactly or misspell the correct term. These can be particularly difficult if you are not familiar enough with material. One way to study for these question types is to create flash cards in which you place terms or major concepts on one side and a definition or description of the term or concept on the other side.

PROBLEM SOLVING. Problem solving or critical thinking questions are used by instructors so that students can demonstrate or apply the concepts or ideas they have learned. When you answer problem solving questions, read the question carefully, marking multiple steps or parts to the directions. Next, determine what information you will need to solve the problem. Then, break the problem into parts and write down what process or operation you will need to perform. Work through the problem, and once you arrive at an answer, check the question again to make sure you have adequately answered it.

Studying for problem solving tests, such as math and science tests, most likely will involve practicing similar problems. Look to the additional problems in your textbook, homework assignments, and notes for extra practice. Also, you may find sample problems much like the ones you are studying for online, with answers provided so that you can check yourself.

GRIT
Instinct

Problem solving is largely a matter of instinct, the kind you can grow. Be a gritty problem solver by asking, "How would the smartest person in the world solve this problem?" or, "What would be a different, potentially better way to go at this?" Try at least two angles and see how well you do!

ESSAY QUESTIONS. Instructors use essay questions to help them measure students' ability to analyze, synthesize, and evaluate the concepts they have learned. This type of question gauges more than students' recall of facts or terms. You can be assured that you will encounter

GRIT GAINER™

GRIT'S GOT GAME There is nothing that can accelerate and strengthen your mastery of tests faster than relentless practice. GRIT matters most on the kinds of tests that are most scary and difficult for you. Spar with others—make it a game. Start simple and build up the intensity, difficulty, and speed.

more essay questions in college because they allow students to demonstrate a deeper understanding of the material. In an exam context, the term *essay* can also refer to questions that require more detailed, well-developed answers that use material from the course to support a particular thesis or describe a particular concept. Your answers to essay questions in an exam should not be based on your own opinion (unless the professor specifically asks for your opinion). Instead, your answer should demonstrate your understanding and recall of important information from the class (e.g., textbook readings, lecture notes) to address a particular challenge or to explain an idea.

One thing to remember about essay questions is that, although you won't have an enormous amount of time to complete an essay, your professor will still expect that you answer the question thoroughly and clearly. Always read the directions carefully. If the essay question has more than one part, be sure to mark each part and answer it in the body of the essay. If the directions specify a length, be sure to meet or exceed it. Before you begin writing, create a brief outline of what you will cover in the essay.

Study for essay questions just as you would problem solving questions by practicing with possible topics. If your professor has provided a list of topics or sample topics, use them to create outlines and memorize those outlines—they will serve as the basis for your essay. If you do not receive any sample topics, create your own by reviewing the course material and your notes to find emphasized topics or material that you spent the most time on. These may be good indications of essay topics.

THE G R I T ADVANTAGE

Growth. Getting good at studying, memorizing, and exams is about effort more than intelligence. Ask yourself, "How can I put in smarter, better effort to learn what I need to learn?"

Resilience. Most students fail to study or prepare for exams because something got in the way. Whenever an obstacle arises, ask yourself, "How can I get past this as quickly as possible so I can get on with my studies?"

Instinct. Ask yourself before every test, "What would be the best, most effective and efficient way for me to prepare for this challenge?"

Tenacity. As you practice different test questions, by yourself and with others, keep repeating, "Again! Again!" until you've got it down cold, and you're ready for prime time.

HOW **GRITTY** ARE YOU?

Now that you've completed this chapter, how committed are you to:

1. Changing how you study so you can enjoy better results?

    Zero Commitment 0 ———————————————————————— 10 **Fully Committed**

2. Practicing before tests and exams to improve your ability and confidence?

    Zero Commitment 0 ———————————————————————— 10 **Fully Committed**

3. Applying these tools to enhance your memory and performance in school?

    Zero Commitment 0 ———————————————————————— 10 **Fully Committed**

4. Sacrificing, even struggling, to do what it takes to study and do well?

    Zero Commitment 0 ———————————————————————— 10 **Fully Committed**

9 Communication and Diversity

Chapter goals to help you get in, get through, get out, and get paid:

In order to get in, get through, get out, and get paid, you will need to get along well with others, including students, faculty, and staff who have different backgrounds, experiences, and perspectives than you. You'll need to learn how to thrive in a diverse environment to be successful in college, your career, and your life.

To meet those goals, this chapter will help you:

- Tailor your communication to accommodate a diverse audience
- Create and participate in teams
- Manage conflict in one-on-one and team settings
- Appreciate the diversity in how people show and apply their **GRIT**

MyStudentSuccessLab™

Log in to MyStudentSuccessLab.com to deepen your **GRIT** mindset and build the skills you'll need to get through the college experience.

Michael's Story

© MONKEY BUSINESS IMAGES/SHUTTERSTOCK

"Evan, are you going to be around later today? I may need some help," Michael asks.

One reason Michael felt an instant connection with Evan that first day they met was that Evan is a lot like him.

"Sure, man," Evan says. "Maybe you can help me, too. You think you can lend me a hand with some furniture?"

"Are you sure you can use help from an old man like me?" Michael asks. Michael has never thought much about being a nontraditional student until recently, when some students he is working with on a group project said something about his being "too old" to work with.

"You may be old, man, but I'm pretty sure you can bench press more than me," Evan says as he laughs.

"Maybe when I was your age, but not anymore," Michael says. "Seriously, though, I have this group project, and, well, my group keeps meeting without me."

"Ah, c'mon," Evan says. "I would make you the leader of my group."

"I think that is part of the problem, too," Michael says. "I don't know, maybe I come on too strong, offend people."

"So what do you need from me? Need some boxing tips?" Evan asks.

"Do you think I should talk to the professor?" asks Michael.

"Man, what do you have to lose by asking?" Evan replies.

Now, what do you think?

- What would you do if you were left out of a group assignment?
  - **a.** Ignore the snub and complete the project on my own
  - **b.** Get the professor to intervene on my behalf
  - **c.** Reach out to my group and ask what I can do to contribute

- If you wanted to be sure that you don't experience this again, what would you do?
  - **a.** Cultivate relationships on the first day of class
  - **b.** Do nothing—not everyone will be excited to work with me all the time
  - **c.** Alert the professor to past problems with group work and ask for an alternative assignment

Your Communication Needs to Match a Diverse Audience

In college, as in life, our ability to communicate with one another is one of the most important skills that we can develop. People who can listen to and understand the ideas and feelings of others, and who can effectively communicate their own ideas and feelings, are able to succeed in life and maintain healthy relationships. On the other hand, people who have a difficult time communicating or who aren't effective at listening to and understanding others often find themselves struggling to navigate the challenges and opportunities in life. To put it more simply, your ability to communicate—verbally and in written form, listening and speaking—is one of the most important skills that you can develop during your college experience.

To understand the communication process, break it down into the "who," "what," "how," and "why." "Who" are the people who are communicating—the sender and receiver (or senders and receivers, if the communication is in a group setting). "What" is the message—the actual content and meaning of what the sender is trying to convey to the receiver. "How" is the method used by the sender to convey the message and its meaning, and might include written messages, the spoken word, or nonverbal communication such as facial expressions, gestures, or tone of voice. "Why" is the intent and motive of the sender. All of us can probably remember a time in our lives when we spoke or wrote something with the intent of hurting

It's in the syllabus

Review your syllabus and determine what information is provided that will help you better communicate with your professor.

- What are the professor's office hours?
- How does your professor prefer to be contacted when you have a question?
- What are the expectations regarding meeting with your professors?

EXHIBIT 9.1	**The Four Questions of Communication**
Who?	With whom am I communicating?
What?	What is the content and meaning I intend to convey?
How?	What method is best for this particular message?
Why?	Why am I communicating this message? What is my intent and motivation?

someone's feelings, but we can also remember times when we were trying to help someone, but the receiver reacted to the message with hurt feelings. Such situations help us realize that our intent influences how and what we communicate, but we don't have complete control over the receiver's interpretation of our message. See Exhibit 9.1 for the four key communication questions.

In light of the "who," "what," "how," and "why" of communication, one of the challenges and opportunities in college is to learn how to modify and adjust your communication to match your audience (or the receiver). In college, you will engage in communication with other students, professors, staff, administrators, and employers, as well as your friends, family, and other loved ones. On any given day, you will find yourself communicating with very different people in very different situations, and it will be helpful to learn how to adjust your communication to help you achieve your goals and intent. To prepare yourself for effectively communicating with diverse audiences, let's explore what diversity is and how it might occur on your campus.

■ Developing cultural competence means learning to appreciate diversity.

© MIKE FLIPPO/SHUTTERSTOCK

Value Diversity and Develop Your Cultural Competence

An exciting part of college is that you will meet and work with people from all ages and backgrounds. Universities attract individuals from a wide variety of backgrounds with a broad spectrum of opinions and beliefs. Your college experience offers a great opportunity for you to learn how to live, learn, and work with other people who may be very different from you in some ways, but who share similarities with you as well. A simple definition of diversity is "difference" or "variety." Another term heard when diversity is discussed in a college setting is *multiculturalism*. Although the two words have different implications, they often have the same motivation—to expose the community to a variety of ideas, cultures, viewpoints, beliefs, and backgrounds.

Recognize and Appreciate Gender and Sexual Orientation Diversity

You will encounter gender diversity at your college, and what this means for you is that you will have plenty of opportunities to work with both men and women and explore any preconceptions you may have about the differences between the sexes.

integrity matters

Integrity is related to trust. You want to be able to trust others, and you want to be someone who is trustworthy. As you build friendships in college, your friends might share something about themselves that is private or sensitive, such as their sexual orientation. How you handle that information will greatly affect your relationship with that person and whether people consider you trustworthy.

YOUR TURN

In approximately 250 words, describe a time in which you demonstrated your trustworthiness by being discreet about information that someone shared with you. Discuss the effects of the experience and how you felt about it.

You may have to pay more attention to society's assumptions about gender and be more attuned to how language, art, and sciences, among other disciplines, perpetuate gender stereotypes.

Sexual orientation is another type of diversity that you will more than likely encounter in college, if you have not already. Homosexuality and bisexuality are just two categories of sexual orientation diversity. Organizations such as the Human Rights Campaign (www.hrc.org) strive to educate others about discrimination that can—and does—occur because of the stereotypes and prejudice that exist regarding sexual orientation. Why should you know more about sexual orientation as a part of diversity? Sexuality is part of the human experience, and one purpose of higher education is to help you better understand and appreciate your and others' human experience. Recognizing sexual orientation as a category of diversity gives you a more complete picture of humankind.

Tenacity

Ask yourself, "Over the past several months, who have I tried and failed to really connect with?" Then try two more times, in different ways, to see if you can forge the beginning of a relationship you might enjoy.

Racial, Ethnic, and Cultural Diversity Enables Cultural Competence

The demographic profile of our planet is changing in dramatic ways that affect you wherever you live. The population growth among countries like China and India, the increase in the U.S. Hispanic population, and the growth of the world's Muslim population are just a few examples of demographic trends that will affect not only your college experience, but also your career and personal life well beyond college. Learning to communicate and work well with individuals who have a different demographic profile than your own is a critical skill for lifelong learning.

The university environment also provides the ideal place for you to meet people of diverse cultures and backgrounds. Be proactive and seek out these opportunities whenever possible. It may seem intimidating at first, especially if you recognize that you're lacking in certain aspects of cultural competence. But just as the citizens of a foreign country appreciate it when a visitor attempts to speak in their language—even if it's done somewhat poorly—the people of different cultures with whom you engage will welcome and appreciate your efforts to learn more about them and their perspectives.

Resilience

Everyone can benefit by diversifying one's relationships and perspectives. Sometimes you have to create a little adversity for yourself by asking, "Who—what person or group—makes me the most uncomfortable? How can I overcome my discomfort to connect and expand my perspective?"

Instinct

People from different backgrounds have learned to handle hardships, stressors, and challenges in different ways. Tap their wisdom by asking for their advice on how to handle yours as they arise.

Generational Diversity

You will, no doubt, encounter generational diversity at your college and in the world of work—more so than in generations past. A generational cohort is a group of the population that was born within a certain period of time, that mark some of the same world events as important, and that hold certain common values (Zemke et al., 2000). Generational cohorts hold certain values that influence how they work with others and how they achieve personal success. During your college experience, you will have classmates, professors, employers, coworkers, or friends from a different generation than your own, and this creates a wonderful opportunity to learn how to work with someone who has a different perspective on life than you do. The key with generational diversity—as with all types of diversity—is to learn more about yourself and others and appreciate the differences.

Socioeconomic Diversity Shouldn't Be Overlooked

The forms of diversity we've discussed so far—gender, ethnic, racial, cultural, and generational—tend to be observable characteristics. However, there are other forms of diversity that are less visible, but no less important, such as socioeconomic diversity. Students, faculty, staff, and administrators come from a wide variety of social and economic backgrounds, and this variety provides yet another enrichment opportunity for your college experience.

■ Your institution may provide you exposure to a variety of different people.

© MONKEY BUSINESS IMAGES/ SHUTTERSTOCK

Because of differences in socioeconomic background, the student sitting next to you may have a very different set of beliefs, attitudes, abilities, experiences, and motivations than you do. These differences may have little to do with his physical characteristics and far more to do with his childhood experiences in a relatively poor or wealthy family. To help you explore this dimension of diversity even more, we encourage you to take a look at the book *Bridges Out of Poverty* by Ruby K. Payne, Philip De-Vol, and Terie Dreussi Smith.

Adjusting Your Communication to Accommodate Diversity

Now that we have a more complete perspective on the types of diversity you might encounter on your campus, the question is how you might need to adjust your communication to accommodate differences. You'll recall the "who," "what," "how," and "why" of

GRIT GAINER™

BE DIFFERENT, BE GRITTY Because people are often scared of or hesitant with people who are different from themselves, you have to A) be the one who initiates the effort to connect with people different from you, and B) often try multiple times, in various ways, to make it work.

Meeting
expectations

The college will expect that I . . .	To meet that expectation, I will . . .
Example: . . . value diversity of viewpoints and perspectives.	*Example:* . . . listen to others' ideas with an open mind so that I can understand their points of view, even if they are different than my own.

communication that we discussed earlier. As you encounter diversity, you'll see that "who" you are communicating with might lead you to adjust "what" you say or write, "how" you say or write it, and "why" you are communicating in the first place. For example, let's take the difference between communicating with your professor and communicating with one of your classmates via email. When you're sending emails to your classmates, you might use conversational forms of expression and an informal style of communicating because it reflects how you would talk to the classmate if he or she was sitting next to you in class. On the other hand, if you are communicating with your professor via email, you would be well-advised to communicate in a more formal manner, proofread your writing, use full sentences and avoid abbreviations or slang, and convey a respect for authority. Because the "who" is different, so will be the "what," "how," and "why" of your communication.

In the same manner, when you are communicating with individuals who are different from you in terms of any aspect of diversity (e.g., gender, ethnicity, socioeconomic background), you will want to adjust your communication to help ensure that the person with whom you are communicating will fully understand the meaning that you are trying to convey and to prevent the person from misinterpreting your intent.

If all of this talk about adjusting your communication to accommodate a diverse audience has you nervous that you might say something wrong, don't worry. If you make the effort to learn about people who are different from you, spend time with them, and talk with them, you'll develop great relationships. Just by being thoughtful and considerate of how someone else might be different from you will help you immensely. Recognizing that someone may not understand English as well as you do or that someone is older or younger than you are will help you recognize that you will need to adjust your communication accordingly. The most important factor is that in recognizing differences, you are also respecting these differences and making the extra effort to communicate effectively.

Success in College Is a Team Effort

Teamwork is a term you've probably heard a lot, and it probably generates a mixed response on your part. In some ways, teams provide a great experience because you can complete projects, compete in events, and experience various activities in a social setting, sharing work and responsibilities along the way. On the other hand, team experiences can be challenging when individual team members have conflicts with each other or when certain team members disrupt the group's efforts or don't fulfill their responsibilities.

Whatever feelings you might have about teams, the most important realization is that your future success in your personal life and career will depend, in large part, on your ability to work well in a team. Whether you aspire to be a doctor, lawyer, veterinarian, teacher,

the unwritten rules
of Communication and Diversity

- **Students who learn to communicate with diverse audiences are better equipped to succeed in life and their careers.** If you attend a campus that is extremely diverse by any definition, the practice and experience you'll gain from learning to communicate in this environment will set you up well for future success. Conversely, if you're on a campus that tends to lack diversity, look for opportunities to engage with diverse audiences by participating in activities that may be outside your comfort zone. The extra effort will yield rewards later.

- **Working on a project with a team will take more time, but will also yield a better project than an individual effort.** You may encounter some difficult team situations that make you wonder if it would be easier to just do the project on your own. In the long run, a project that's been developed by a team always tends to be a better project than an individual effort. That's why so many companies and professionals use teams to accomplish their objectives.

- **The most common mistake that people make in conflict resolution is bringing other people into the conflict too early.** People have a tendency to want to talk about a problem with everyone but the person with whom they have the problem. This will only complicate the problem and escalate the conflict. Once you have identified the problem, take time to have a one-on-one conversation with the person you're having the conflict with. It may be a tough conversation, but it'll be worth it.

Resilience

Like success, GRIT is not always a solo act. As you join with a diverse group of people, consider seeking those who are most resilient, who have struggled the most but shine brightest when adversity strikes. Those are the kind of people you can count on to get stuff done.

professional athlete, social worker, or website developer, you will be working in teams. And given the increasing use of technology like videoconferencing and social media, the dispersion of technical workers across the globe, and the shifting demographic trends in the United States, it is likely that you will be working in teams that span different cultures, geographies, and career specialties. In other words, you will undoubtedly be working in teams that consist of people who have different backgrounds and perspectives and who may even live somewhere else on the planet.

So, how do you succeed in a team environment? First, review the information that you have received from your instructor about the project and the expectations. Having a clear understanding of what your goal is will make it easier to begin your work as a team. You will also want to note the expectations for the teamwork. For example, will the team members be assigned roles? Will each team member evaluate each other at the conclusion of the project? Get clarification from your professor now instead of waiting until later in the semester. Sometimes it makes sense to assign team members to certain responsibilities based on their experiences or interests. For example, one of your team members might be an exceptional writer, so that person might be the best choice to format and proofread each version of the paper. You also need to designate one or two team members who will assume the primary leadership role in overseeing the project and its completion.

Next, meet early in the term and establish a regular meeting schedule for your team. Compare schedules and find a recurring time (e.g., every Thursday from 11:00 A.M.–noon) when every team member is expected to attend. Many teams wait too long for their first meetings, but even if a project isn't due until the end of the term, it's far better to meet early in the term to set a course for success on the project or assignment.

When your team is first established, develop a communication system so that everyone on the team always knows what is happening. One suggestion is to have someone on the team take notes during every meeting (this responsibility could rotate among team members) and distribute those notes via email immediately after every meeting. It's best to communicate with each other clearly and often, preferably in writing. Then, identify both goals and deadlines for your team. What do you have to accomplish and when? Confirming these goals and deadlines in writing will help bring the team together towards a shared purpose.

Once your team is established, schedule regular team meetings with your professor. Initially, you can review the assignment or project requirements with your professor to make sure that everyone has the same understanding about the assignment. Then, you can meet with your professor to review a first or second draft of your paper or project, giving the professor a chance to offer feedback that you can respond to before the formal due date. You might also need to meet with your professor to help you resolve team conflicts that might emerge. Build enough lead time into your timeline to develop first drafts of your written assignments or oral presentations and to finalize the final version of your work. Some professors will be willing to read initial drafts and provide preliminary feedback, which can really help you improve your final version. Drafts can also give your team some time to review it yourself and refine it before turning in the final copy. Rehearsing your presentation well in advance of the formal presentation date will also lead to a much better final version (and a better grade) than if you wait until the last minute to finalize the paper or prepare the presentation.

Decide as a team to approach your tasks and challenges with a gritty mindset. Use your GRIT and ask yourselves, "How can we use this assignment to help each of us grow?" Then support each other in making that happen.

Finally, develop a process—before any conflicts occur—for how you will resolve conflicts when they do occur. In general, if a conflict occurs between two team members, those two individuals should attempt to resolve the conflict directly before bringing the issue to the attention of other team members. If the two team members cannot resolve the conflict, they should bring the conflict to the team as a whole, and the team leaders should attempt to facilitate some kind of resolution. If the team leaders are unsuccessful in their efforts, the team should schedule a meeting with the professor to fully discuss the issue and seek the professor's help in resolving the situation. By following this "lowest level of conflict" approach and starting with the two people in conflict, most problems can be quickly and easily resolved without requiring involvement from the entire team.

By implementing these recommendations in any team, whether it's at school, home, or work, you will discover that you can accomplish a lot more—and better—work than individually. Teams are powerful and, with the right management approach, can be quite effective as well.

Conflict Will Happen, but You Can Resolve It

While you are in college, you may find yourself in a conflict that must be resolved in order for you to be successful and satisfied. The conflict can arise between you and a family member, a classmate, a roommate, or even a professor. How you handle the conflict may have long-term consequences for your success. Often a minor conflict such as miscommunication or a misunderstanding can easily be resolved. Other times, the disagreement may require more time and effort and the help of others.

Conflict is a given. How you approach it is up to you. Show some GRIT. Agree as a team that you will dig deep and do whatever it takes to resolve any conflicts that can impede your goal.

Boundaries Provide Healthy Limits

Because you will be surrounded by a diverse group of people, it may be difficult for you to create and maintain the traditional boundaries that exist between students and their counselors, professors, administrators, and learning support staff. What is a boundary?

© DIEGO CERVO/FOTOLIA

Learning to work well with others and complete tasks as a team, regardless of how different they are from you, is an important skill to develop in college.

As Cloud and Townsend (1992) explain, a *boundary* is a property line that defines the beginning and end of what we own and what others own. In the context of relationships, it helps us understand who owns—or is responsible for—feelings, attitudes, and behaviors. It almost seems contradictory, but boundaries are necessary when you are getting to know others. Why should you refrain from close relationships with professors and advisors when you need them to get to know you if you are to ask for a referral or recommendation?

For one, some colleges discourage intimately personal relationships between professors and students, just as many companies prohibit the same type of overly friendly relationship between supervisors and their employees because such relationships can be problematic. One possible problem is that intimate relationships can result in perceived or actual unfair evaluation or treatment. Because a professor is considered a superior, the college views the professor's role as one of authority and power. Many sexual harassment policies and laws are built on the imbalance of power between a person in authority and a subordinate.

G R I T
Tenacity

Setting and sticking to boundaries takes tenacity. People will challenge or violate them, even unintentionally. Use your GRIT to set and honor the boundaries that belong in your relationships.

Problems Require Procedures

No matter how well you define your boundaries and work hard to maintain good relationships with those around you, conflicts will occur. Universities tend to have well-established processes and procedures to help students, professors, and staff members successfully resolve almost any kind of conflict; it's helpful to be familiar with these as well as to establish some processes and procedures that you'll use personally. Knowing and following these procedures will ensure that a problem is handled appropriately and quickly.

The first step to resolving a conflict in class is to define the problem. Is it a communication problem? Is it a problem with the grading standards in a course? Do you feel like a team member is not fulfilling his responsibilities? When you're defining the problem, be sure to acknowledge anything that you did to contribute to it. Conflicts can often be disarmed simply by having both people acknowledge their mistakes and express a desire to resolve the problem.

Once you have defined the problem, your next step is to discuss the problem with the person directly. If the problem is with your instructor, make an appointment during her office hours to discuss the issue. If the conflict is with a classmate, set up a time to discuss the issue one-on-one without interruptions or distractions. If you are emotional—angry, upset, nervous—wait until you have calmed down to discuss the problem.

For the process of conflict resolution to work, you will need to complete these first two steps. If you are not satisfied with the result or if you feel the problem has gotten worse, not better, move to the next step: bringing others into the situation to help

G R I T
Resilience

Problem solving takes GRIT. Focus together on minimizing the downside and getting through any problems as quickly and completely as possible. Those who respond better and faster, win!

GRIT GAINER™

GOT CONFLICT? USE GRIT   School is the perfect place to hone the skills that will help you succeed in the rest of your life. Practice using your GRIT to work through the most difficult problems and conflicts by asking:

- "How can we approach this conflict in a way that honors and benefits everyone?"
- "How can we come at this better/differently to produce a less frustrating and more positive result?"
- "What else can we try to at least increase the chances this works out well for everyone?"

resolve it. If your conflict is with a professor, this will involve the department chair or dean. If your conflict is with one of your roommates, the next step is to bring other roommates into the conversation. Again, your goal at this step is to resolve the issue. Stay focused on the specific problem that you defined in step 1, and try to maintain a calm, respectful attitude as you work through the conflict. If your efforts to resolve conflict with your professor are unsuccessful, even after consulting with the department head or dean, your last stop is with the dean of students or vice president for academic affairs. Starting at the top will only delay resolution.

THE GRIT GRIT ADVANTAGE

Put this chapter to immediate use with these two tips:

1. Pick the three to five people from whom you think you could learn the most or to whom you could contribute the most. Using the tips in this chapter, mentally sketch out your approach and message. How will you best communicate with each of them, given their uniqueness and differences?

2. Pick the one conflict in your life that bothers you the most and give it your best shot to resolve it constructively to the benefit of everyone involved.

HOW GRITTY ARE YOU?

Now that you've completed this chapter, how committed are you to:

1. Dealing with the discomfort and frustration you sometimes feel when dealing with people different from you in order to build more diverse relationships?

   Zero Commitment **0** ———————————————————— **10** Fully Committed

2. Being more sensitive to and putting much more effort into how you connect and communicate with people who may be different from you?

   Zero Commitment **0** ———————————————————— **10** Fully Committed

3. Digging deep and doing whatever it takes to resolve your conflicts as constructively as possible?

   Zero Commitment **0** ———————————————————— **10** Fully Committed

10 Information Literacy

Chapter goals to help you *get in, get through, get out, and get paid:*

In order to get in, get through, get out, and get paid, you'll need to gather and use information effectively to support your arguments. These skills will also be very important in your career after college, so your hard work will pay off for a lifetime.

To meet those goals, *this chapter will help you:*

- Appreciate the importance of information literacy
- Identify appropriate sources of information
- Evaluate information for its reliability, credibility, currency, and accuracy
- Use ideas and information ethically
- Demonstrate the **GRIT** it takes to put the tools from this chapter to use

MyStudentSuccessLab™

Log in to MyStudentSuccessLab.com to deepen your **GRIT** mindset and build the skills you'll need to get through the college experience.

Juanita's Story

©ANDRESR/SHUTTERSTOCK

"A 15-page research paper and five-minute PowerPoint presentation. Due during the last week of class," Juanita repeats to her mother over the phone.

"What do you have to write it on?" her mother asks.

"We get to pick from a list, but I don't even know what some of the topics are, like 'conflict management theory,'" Juanita says as she looks over the list again. "I guess that is the point of research."

"You better get started, Juanita. I know how you are about writing papers—even when you end up doing well." Juanita remembered many nights she stayed up writing papers at the last minute because she didn't know how to get started. She also felt she did better during the excitement of the clock ticking.

"I guess this is my chance to break those bad habits," Juanita says.

"I thought this was sociology, not English," her mother says.

"It is, Mom, but all of my instructors still expect me to write a good paper," Juanita says. "And it is not just a paper. I have to get up and say something about what I learned. You know how nervous I get doing that."

Juanita heads toward the library to start writing her 15-page paper and creating a presentation on a topic that she knows nothing about right now.

Now, what do you think?

- What would you do if you were unsure how to start an assignment?
    a. Not worry; I will find a classmate to help me
    b. Do what I usually do—wait until a few days before to start or get help
    c. Start planning now to understand the assignment and start on it
- What strategies could you use to ensure that you can tackle future writing and researching assignments?
    a. Practice writing and researching repeatedly
    b. Use the feedback I get from my professors to focus on what I can improve
    c. Nothing—I am either a good writer or not, and no amount of extra effort will change that

Information Literacy Prepares You for Success

As your college experience kicks into high gear, one of the many adjustments you will have to face is the dramatic increase in the amount of information you need to process. Whether you are a part- or full-time student, you will be attending classes, researching assignments, processing information about your degree plan and eventually your career plan, and handling information about financial aid, graduation requirements, and other content that pertains to your college experience. This information will come at you in the form of textbooks, articles, websites, emails, discussion boards, podcasts, lectures, forums, Twitter feeds, Facebook posts, flyers, announcements, and a variety of other forms of information.

Your ability to handle this information and use it effectively to make decisions and succeed in college will depend on your information literacy. Information literacy "is the set of skills needed to find, retrieve, analyze, and use information" (American Library Association, 2012). To become truly information literate, you will need to become proficient at finding information, understanding and evaluating that information, and using it effectively to complete important assignments and make important decisions. These are skills that will serve you throughout your lifetime, not just in college.

See Exhibit 10.1 for the components of information literacy. As the American Library Association Presidential Committee on Information Literacy (1989) explains, "Ultimately, information literate people are those who have learned how to learn. They know how to learn because they know how knowledge is organized, how to find information, and how to use information in such a way that others can learn from them. They are people prepared for lifelong learning, because they can always find the information needed for any task or decision at hand."

EXHIBIT 10.1   What Is Information Literacy?

Skill	Examples
Find	• Navigating the library catalog system to locate a book • Using an Internet search engine to find sources • Referencing a book's index to find coverage of a topic
Retrieve	• Checking out a book from the library or photocopying pages • Downloading articles from the Internet and citing the source properly • Downloading statistical data from the U.S. Census
Analyze	• Using three different sources by three different authors to support the same conclusion • Applying statistical analysis to data to show important patterns • Critiquing an expert's opinion because of weaknesses in his or her argument
Use	• Making recommendations to a business owner based on your research findings • Making a financial decision of your own based on careful research • Using research to make a decision about how to vote during the next election

Ways to Find Appropriate Information Sources

There are a lot of potential sources of information that you might be able to use for an assignment or activity. This information might be in electronic form, printed, or presented orally. Some information is already available and just needs to be located, but other information needs to be generated, such as an interview with an expert on a particular topic.

To avoid getting overwhelmed with the number and variety of potential sources of information, start with the specific assignment, project, or decision at hand. For example, if your purpose for gathering information is to complete a class assignment, then read the syllabus and assignment carefully and talk with your professor about his or her expectations. Your assignment and topic will influence what kinds of sources you will use for your paper. If your education class requires that you find websites that provide information on cyberbullying in elementary schools, then you will know that you can restrict your research to websites. However, if your education class requires that you write a research paper on the latest studies on cyberbullying, you will most likely use multiple sources, such as accessing journals in your library's databases to find articles on the subject and reviewing school and scholarly websites. Some professors will provide specific, detailed guidelines for the types of information sources they want you to use; others may offer only vague instructions. In the latter case, try to spend time with the professor during office hours to get clarification about the kinds of information they would recommend, especially if it's the first assignment you're completing for that professor.

If you are gathering information to help you make a decision, ask yourself what information would really help you. Perhaps you've seen movies like *Mission Impossible* in which the agents use computers to acquire instantaneous information to help them complete their mission. Imagine, for a moment, that you had that kind of access to

G R I T
Tenacity

Research sometimes requires tremendous focus and dedication. But when you dig deep and do it right, it can save you a ton of time and help you hand in a top-notch assignment.

It's in the
syllabus

The syllabus can provide information about writing expectations for your class in the course outline, assignments, or grading sections.

• What are the expectations for writing assignments in your class?

• Does the syllabus outline these expectations or provide grading criteria?

• If you are unclear of the expectations for writing in your classes, how can you find out more information?

• What resources are available to help you determine what to expect?

© LITHIAN/FOTOLIA

■ Prepare for a writing assignment by thinking about what you need and want to write about and what sources you will need to use.

information—what would you want to have in front of you to help you make an informed decision? Typically, this information would help you identify all of your alternatives, the trade-offs of each alternative, and the likelihood of success if you choose one alternative over another.

Once you have a good sense of the kinds of information you would like to have for your assignment or decision, then you can begin to identify and evaluate potential sources of that information. It is at this point in the research process that many of your peers will instinctively jump on the Internet and start to use Google or another search engine to find their sources of information. Although this may be a useful strategy in some cases, it is rarely your best option, so try to avoid copying everyone else with this approach. Instead, consider the following sources of information based on their potential usefulness, relevance, and reliability:

- Start by consulting your campus library, either in person or via the website, to see if they offer helpful research guides or directories that list the various sources of information you could use for an assignment or decision. Exhibit 10.2 shows a sample research guide from a university librarian that serves as a useful starting point for any research project related to marketing.

- Thinking back to the *Mission Impossible* scenario, determine what information you would ideally like to have in front of you to help you write a paper or complete a project. Would financial data, statistics, or other numeric information be most helpful, or do you need authoritative opinions or explanations of certain concepts or ideas? Your library will have specific sources that relate to both types of information. Knowing what you want in advance will aid your search.

- If possible, use library databases to locate peer-reviewed sources of information, such as academic and scientific journals. When something is *peer reviewed* it means that the author's work was carefully reviewed, challenged, and supported by other experts in the field. These sources may be difficult to understand, but their summaries might offer some clues about their potential usefulness for your assignment. Their primary benefit is that they provide information that has a high degree of credibility because of the scientific methods used to conduct the research and the reputation of the experts who write the articles.

- Government agencies, such as the Bureau of Labor Statistics (bls.gov) and the Census Bureau (census.gov), provide a trove of data and information pertaining to a wide variety of topics. By using data from these sources, you are providing authoritative support for your findings and opinions. When you locate useful data and information, be sure to take careful notes about the source so that you can provide an accurate bibliography.

- Look for journals, magazines, and newspapers that are well known and widely read, such as the *New York Times*, *The Wall Street Journal*, *Time*, *Newsweek*, and *National Geographic*, just to name a few. Articles from these sources will be easier to read and understand than academic journals, but still provide a high level of credibility because of the reputation of these publications.

- Websites are obviously a useful source of information about topics, but always look for evidence that there is a specific authoritative source or author whom you can reference as the source of the information.

G R I T
Instinct

The difference between decent information and the best information is often a matter of GRIT. Ask yourself, "Where haven't I yet looked that might offer some new, different, hopefully better and/or important insight?"

EXHIBIT 10.2   **Sample Research Guide**

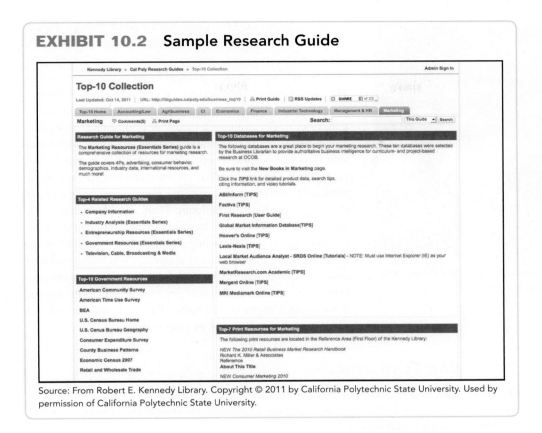

Source: From Robert E. Kennedy Library. Copyright © 2011 by California Polytechnic State University. Used by permission of California Polytechnic State University.

- Depending on the project and your professor's assignment, you may also need to generate your own sources of information or data. For example, you may need or want to interview experts on particular topics to gather their opinions and experiences. Or, if you need numerical data, you may need to conduct your own study, such as comparing the prices of groceries across several supermarkets.

Because there are so many potential sources and types of information, it's always best to seek some guidance and clarification from your professor before embarking on your research project. Finding authoritative sources of information and data that support your primary conclusions and arguments will greatly improve the quality of your work and, ultimately, your grade.

Make Sure Your Sources Are Reliable, Credible, Current, and Accurate

Once you find your sources, you will need to spend time deciding if they are reliable, credible, and useable for your paper. Again, look to your assignment or to your professor for guidance if you are unsure whether the source is acceptable. Most likely, if it is a source that you have found in the library's catalog or databases, it should be credible.

Use Your Sources to Support Your Argument or Thesis

Once you've located sources that provide reliable and relevant information for your paper, you can use these sources to organize, strengthen, and support your argument or thesis. A research paper is different from an essay because an essay relies primarily on your own opinion, whereas a research paper draws on outside sources to support your point.

■ Learning how to use sources ethically will help you become truly information literate.

What types of advertisements or news articles do you believe are the most persuasive? Chances are you consider ads or articles that use factual data, expert sources, and logical arguments to support their point to be particularly persuasive. The same approach applies to your research paper. If the purpose of your paper is to argue a point, make a recommendation, or critically evaluate a theory or philosophy, your paper will have a stronger argument if you can support it with verifiable facts and outside sources. Once you've written a draft of your research paper, carefully review it and use a highlighter to mark every statement that someone might argue against or any claim that someone might doubt. Then, consider whether you can find an outside source to support your argument or claim. For example, if you're writing a report about the effect of the BP oil spill on the Gulf Coast economy, you could find economic data and quotes from industry experts to support your claims that the oil spill caused negative effects to the region. Your research paper will be better if you can provide research support for most, if not all, of your claims.

Evaluating Your Sources

Once you've located several sources of information and reviewed the information provided by each source, it's a good idea to take some time to evaluate the information for its reliability, credibility, currency, and accuracy:

- **Reliability.** Reliability tends to mean that the source of information is consistent over time. A tape measure, for example, provides a reliable measure of length every time you use it. On the other hand, commentary on TV news channels about a breaking news story might change rapidly as new information emerges. Blogs, Twitter feeds, Facebook posts, and other social media sources are often quite informative for fast-moving stories, but they won't be as reliable as other sources of information that will remain consistent over time.

- **Credibility.** Is the author or source of the information an authoritative expert on this topic? What is their occupation, title, or background? Have they written a lot of published articles about this topic before?

- **Currency.** How recent is the information? If you're studying the Civil War, it's quite acceptable that the sources of information might be quite old. If you're writing a paper about genetically modified crops, however, you will want to make sure you are drawing on information that was published within the last few years.

GRIT GAINER™

GET GRITTY WITH RESEARCH   Good research requires plenty of GRIT. With each assignment, ask yourself:

1. Where can I get the best and most credible information on this subject?

2. How can I dig deeper to unearth something new about this topic?

3. Where haven't I looked that might offer some brilliant insights on this subject?

- **Accuracy.** The best way to judge the accuracy of information from one source or article is to locate other sources that provide similar information. If two or more sources provide similar data or information, you can have greater confidence in the accuracy of the information.

To evaluate each source of information is a demonstration of your critical thinking skills. It means that you take time to consider whether information is reliable, credible, current, and accurate before you use it to make a decision, reach a conclusion, or support an argument. The ability to think critically about the information you receive and use in college will serve you for a lifetime.

Use Your Sources Ethically

When you find a source that you plan to use in your paper, you need to catalog information about that source. How you do this will depend on the documentation style that your professor requires. Two of the most common are MLA (Modern Language Association) and APA (American Psychological Association), but there are more that you will need to be familiar with: Chicago Manual of Style (CMS) and Council of Biology Editors (CBE) are just two additional ones. A documentation style simply means the format in which you acknowledge your sources within your paper and in the references or works cited page. Your library will have information that can help you use these formats appropriately, and there are several websites, such as the American Library Association (www.ala.org), that provide the information as well.

Regardless of which style you use, incorporating sources into your paper requires that you provide essential information, usually the author's name and the title of the source, whenever you first use it in your paper. This means that whether you are quoting directly or paraphrasing,

the unwritten rules
for Information Literacy

- **A majority of your classmates will fall for the Google trap.** Don't be one of them. You can distinguish yourself as an exceptional student by demonstrating an ability and willingness to search for sources of information that aren't retrieved from a Google search.

- **Information literacy is a great skill to emphasize in job interviews.** If you're interviewing for a part-time job, internship, or your full-time career, demonstrating your ability to find, analyze, evaluate, and use information can set you apart. Every job and every career requires some form of information literacy.

- **You may encounter some tricky situations when you critically evaluate information.** In some situations, your professor might present information in a lecture that you later discover is either outdated or factually incorrect. Before you bring such errors to your professor's attention,

make sure you have authoritative sources of information to back you up, and then schedule time to meet with the professor during office hours. This is a better option than attempting to correct the professor publicly in class.

- **Quality trumps quantity.** Unless your professor has specific guidelines for the number of sources you should use, you will be better served if you find fewer, high-quality sources of information rather than a trove of unreliable sources.

- **Use direct quotes sparingly.** Direct quotes are your nuclear option, so to speak. Only use them when you don't think you can possibly paraphrase what the person is saying. Otherwise, paraphrase the information and cite the source. Papers that are full of direct quotes give the appearance that the author isn't thinking for himself.

which is putting the author's ideas into your own words, you will need to let your reader know where the information comes from. Proper acknowledgment and documentation are essential to incorporating your sources correctly. Your professor will certainly want to hear your thoughts on the topic, but she will also expect that you have found sources to support your ideas and documented them properly.

Be Sure to Avoid Plagiarism

Instinct

Being an ethical writer means taking the high road and avoiding sleazy shortcuts, no matter what—even when you're under the gun on a deadline.

Plagiarism is the act of using someone else's words, images, and ideas without properly and accurately acknowledging them. This definition can also cover artwork and computer programming code. Basically, any material that you use within an assignment, excluding information that is considered common knowledge, must be properly and accurately acknowledged. That means you must be familiar with and use the correct documentation format that your professor requires.

Any time that you are creating, writing, or producing an assignment, either as an individual or as part of a group, you will need to document the information and sources you use. If your professor wants the assignment to be completely original—without the use of sources—then you will need to adhere to those guidelines. If you are completing an assignment as part of a group, you may be asked to document which group members completed which parts of the assignment.

The following is a list of specific instances of plagiarism to avoid in all of your assignments:

- Buying or downloading a paper off the Internet and turning it in as your own
- Copying and pasting material from the Internet or print sources without acknowledging or properly documenting the source
- Allowing someone else to write all or part of your paper
- Creating a "patchwork" of unacknowledged material in your paper by copying words, sentences, or paragraphs from someone else and changing only a few words
- Including fictitious references in your paper

The simplest rule to remember when it comes to plagiarism is that if you had to look up the information or you used part or all of someone else's idea, image, or exact words, you must let your professor or reader know. As in every unclear situation you may encounter, always ask for clarification. Your professor will be able to help you determine what you need to do if you are unsure.

Meeting
expectations

The college will expect that I . . .	To meet that expectation, I will . . .
Example: . . . use information ethically in my papers and presentations.	*Example:* . . . acknowledge all sources of information I have used.

integrity<small>matters</small>

At no time should you copy another student's answers. Just as you would not share answers during a test, it is best not to share your answers on work that is assigned out of class. If you have taken a class in a previous semester, you will also want to keep your assignments from being shared. Instructors may use the same assignments from semester to semester, and you don't want to put a fellow student in an awkward or potentially bad situation.

YOUR TURN

In approximately 250 words, explain how students can compromise academic integrity, perhaps without even knowing it. Then, describe what safeguards students can put in place to ensure academic integrity when working with others, whether it be fellow students or tutors.

THE GRIT ADVANTAGE

Apply these tips to write and research better than ever before:

Growth. Seek new, different information and angles—the stuff most students don't find—to inform your writing and research.

Resilience. Don't play it too safe. Enter the storm by taking the risks that will help you shine.

Instinct. Before you dig in, think about the best way to approach each assignment so you save time and come out with a better result.

Tenacity. Practice harder, do more drafts, and dig deeper than everyone else, and you will amaze yourself with your results!

HOW GRITTY ARE YOU?

Now that you've completed this chapter, how committed are you to:

1. Putting extra time and effort into your writing and research to produce even better results?

   Zero Commitment **0** —————————————————————————————— **10** Fully Committed

2. Seeking the most qualified and brutally honest feedback you can find to accelerate your improvement?

   Zero Commitment **0** —————————————————————————————— **10** Fully Committed

3. Trying over and over until you get skilled at writing and researching?

   Zero Commitment **0** —————————————————————————————— **10** Fully Committed

11 Managing Stress

As you pursue your goals to get in, get through, get out, and get paid, it's a certainty that you'll experience stress. Stress can't be avoided, but it can be managed and even harnessed.

To meet those goals, this chapter will help you:

- Recognize major stressors that affect students
- Take a gritty approach to stress, using it to fuel your performance
- Understand your reaction to personal stressors
- Explore techniques for managing stress
- Develop strategies for maintaining your physical health

MyStudentSuccessLab™

Log in to MyStudentSuccessLab.com to deepen your **GRIT** mindset and build the skills you'll need to get through the college experience.

Evan's Story

© MONKEY BUSINESS IMAGES/SHUTTERSTOCK

Evan was a student by day and a kickboxer by night, usually competing several times a semester. Sometimes he wondered if he could do both and be successful in and out of the ring.

"Evan, man, you're a little late today," his coach said. "What gives? You are usually early to practice."

"Had too much homework to do," Evan replied.

"Evan, I know you are committed to college. That's great, but you have to do your time at the gym."

The words stung Evan. He was highly competitive and was proud of his athletic ability even though he had started to pack on the pounds from too much studying and eating poorly.

Then, there was college—another goal that he wanted to achieve. When he registered for college, he really thought he could do both kickboxing and college and succeed at both.

Evan packed his sweatshirt into his gym bag, stretched, and thought about the homework he still had to complete before going to bed, which was usually about 2:00 A.M. He stopped on the way home to buy a few energy drinks and a protein bar, which would fuel him through his homework for the night.

Now, what do you think?

- If you needed to ensure you had the energy to complete all your goals, what would you do?

  a. Create a balance between what I want to accomplish and taking care of myself physically and emotionally

  b. Give up all but my most pressing goal so I can ensure I can complete it

  c. Use stimulants such as energy drinks and supplements to maintain high energy at all times

- How would you deal with the stress of college demands if you were struggling?

  a. Figure out a way to manage stress on my own

  b. Seek help for managing my stress in the healthiest way

  c. Admit to myself that I cannot do everything and decrease my obligations

Resilience

Stress is determined less by the cause and more by your response. A big part of GRIT is resilience, your capacity to respond to adverse or stressful events in ways that strengthen and improve you. Step 1: Focus on your response. That's where your power lies.

College Has Stressors of Its Own

College offers a lot of new experiences and opportunities that can be fun and exciting, but also stressful. Stress is a physical and psychological response to outside stimuli. In other words, just about anything that stimulates you can cause stress. Not all stress, however, is bad for you. For example, the stress you feel when you see someone get seriously hurt enables you to spring into action to help. For some students, the stress of an upcoming exam gives them the energy and focus to study. Without feeling a little stressed, these students might not feel the need to study at all. In fact, scientific research demonstrates that moderate levels of anxiety enhance performance compared to no anxiety at all—but too much anxiety can be harmful. In other words, a little bit of stress may be good, but too much is not. The key, then, is to manage stress well so it's not overwhelming.

The first step in developing a successful approach for managing stress in college is to identify and anticipate the circumstances and issues in our lives that have the potential to cause stress. The acronym HALT—which stands for hungry, angry, lonely, tired—can also help you anticipate when you might be less resilient to stressful situations.

For example, if you're waiting in line at the bank and you're hungry, you may become more irritable and impatient than if you just enjoyed a good lunch and you're enjoying your favorite coffee while in line. Being aware of times and situations that cause you the most stress is one step in helping manage stress better. In Exhibit 11.1, place an "X" next to situations that are negatively stressful for you. Consider other situations or people that cause you to react negatively.

By understanding the various factors and circumstances in your life that can trigger stress, you can develop an effective stress management plan. The next step is to better understand how you tend to react to these stressors.

Meeting
expectations

The college will expect that I . . .	To meet that expectation, I will . . .
Example: . . . manage my stress in healthy ways.	*Example:* . . . take advantage of college resources to help me maintain my health.
_____	_____
_____	_____
_____	_____

EXHIBIT 11.1   How Stressful Is This Situation?

Situation	Stresses Me	Does Not Stress Me
Starting a big project		
Paying bills		
Being in a messy environment		
Getting back graded papers and exams		
Not getting enough sleep		
Taking a personal or professional risk		
Getting out of bed in the morning		
Not getting feedback on my work		
Being distracted by other people		
Thinking about the future		
Taking tests		

Knowing How You React to Stress Can Help You Manage It

Not everyone handles stress the same way, and what is a stressful situation for you may not be for someone else. How we handle stress depends on our genetic makeup, past experiences, and the stress-reducing techniques that we practice.

When you feel a lot of stress, how do you react? Exhibit 11.2 shows some common types of reactions to stress—some healthy, some unhealthy. As you review this list, take a moment to evaluate (a) how often you react to stressors in this way, and (b) whether this type of reaction is healthy and helpful. This list isn't intended to be exhaustive, so you may react to stress in other ways that aren't mentioned here. The important activity at this stage is to know how you tend to react to stressful situations. Some of your reactions may be helpful and healthy. For example, exercising and spending social time with others talking about your stress can be very helpful. Some of your reactions may be unhelpful and even detrimental to your health. For example, any forms of substance abuse will lead to even greater problems in your life and could seriously harm you.

We all sometimes feel overwhelmed by what we have to accomplish.

© VLUE/SHUTTERSTOCK

EXHIBIT 11.2 Evaluating Reactions to Stressors

Reaction to Stressor	How Often Do You React This Way?			Is This Reaction Healthy and Helpful?	
	Never	Sometimes	Always	Yes	No
Talking to others or venting about a stressful situation, sometimes through Facebook posts or tweets					
Yelling or screaming about the person, situation, or circumstance that is causing the stress					
Going for a walk, practicing yoga, or doing some other form of exercise					
Arguing with others; insulting them, or criticizing them in an effort to "blow off steam"					
Writing in a journal about the experience and the stress and reflecting on why it's triggering such a reaction for you and what caused the stressful circumstance in the first place					
Drinking alcohol or taking drugs					
Praying, meditating, or engaging in some form of spiritual or religious expression					
Eating					
Sleeping					
Escaping from the stressor by going to a movie, listening to music, watching TV, or surfing the web					
Engaging in artistic expression, such as art, music, dance, theater, or graphic design					

integrity matters

Have you ever promised someone that you would do something, only to break your promise? No matter why we break promises, the end result always causes us some stress in our lives because such actions, or inactions, can damage our relationships with others. One way to eliminate stress and anxiety is to make integrity a top priority in your life. Only promise what you know you can deliver; your negative stress will decrease when you maintain your integrity.

YOUR TURN

In approximately 250 words, describe a time when you have let someone down by not delivering on a promise. Discuss how you felt about not honoring your word and how your relationship changed afterwards.

> ### EXHIBIT 11.3   Techniques for Managing Stress
>
> | | |
> |---|---|
> | Practice deep breathing and yoga. | Maintain lines of communication. |
> | Visualize a relaxing place and time. | Maintain flexibility and margin in your schedule and relationships. |
> | Engage in physical activity. | Seek help if it becomes overwhelming. |
> | Find activities tnat make you laugh. | Comfort yourself with familiar favorites. |

To make sure you're on track with your stress management plan, Exhibit 11.3 shows some suggested tips for effectively managing stress.

Resilience

You Can Manage Your Stress

No doubt you have felt stress since enrolling in college. You wouldn't be human if you didn't at least worry at the beginning of the semester how you will manage it all—family, work, college, and a personal life. Stress is normal, but for college students it can seriously derail them from achieving their goals if they cannot manage it successfully. Looking for ways to minimize—not eliminate, because you can't—stress and maximize balance in your life will make your college experience more enjoyable and successful.

> Stress or adversity is when you predict or experience something bad happening to something or someone you care about. This explains why what's stressful to you may or may not be to someone else. It's all about how bad you think it will be and how much you care. The more important it is, and the worse it is, the more stressed you become—unless you create a resilient, gritty response.

Disarm the Negative Effects of Stress

Because you cannot eliminate all stress, you will need to develop methods for reducing the negative effects that your body and mind experience when they are stressed out. One of the quickest, easiest ways to reduce the negative effects of stress is to take a deep breath. You may have even told someone who was upset to breathe deeply in order to calm down. The breath is, as many cultures have known for thousands of years, an important part of life; in yoga, the ability to control the breath is essential to controlling the mind and body.

Tenacity

> One way to take charge of your stress is to "enter the storm." Most people try to avoid or ignore stress. But some stressors or adversities are best handled by dealing with them now, head-on. Rather than worrying about a class, festering over a relationship or issue, or hating a professor, go right to the source to handle it in a constructive way. It beats losing more sleep!

GRIT GAINER™

TAKE CHARGE OF STRESS   Most students do exactly the opposite of what they should do when it comes to stress. They abuse their bodies with junk food, no exercise, poor sleep, and extra caffeine, or worse, right at the time when their bodies crave resilience. Take charge of your stress—funnel it like fuel. Use it to enhance your workouts and focus your mind. Own your stress. Eat healthier than ever, make sleep sacred, and pause for laughter and fun so you can attack your stress with fresh energy.

© 2XSAMARA/SHUTTERSTOCK

■ Minimize the negative effects of stress by scheduling down time to relax or do something you enjoy.

G R I T
Growth

Take a fresh approach to stress. Ask yourself, "What can I do in the next 30 seconds (or 30 minutes) to significantly reduce the downsides of my stress and put me in a grittier mindset?" Confront your stress rather than becoming its victim.

Visualization is another method for reducing the effect that stress has on the mind and body. In order to visualize a more relaxed time and place, all you need to do is to find a quiet, comfortable spot, sit down, and close your eyes. Relaxation experts suggest that you visualize a place that makes you feel warm and relaxed. Many people think about a beach, because the mood there is often relaxed and the sound of the ocean is comforting. You will need to find your own special place.

Once you decide where you want to go mentally, you should start noticing the details in your place. If you are at the beach, then you should feel the sunshine's heat. Next, listen to the waves crashing on the surf and smell the salty air. Depending on how long you need to visualize this special place, you may want to stick your toe in the water or lie down on the beach and soak up the rays—leave your stress in those designated beach trash cans. The goal in this method of relaxation is to stay there as long as you need to; when you mentally return to your present location, you should feel refreshed and renewed.

Sometimes physical activity can be a better stress reliever than mental exercises. Getting outside or to the gym to work out your frustrations is an excellent way of maintaining your health. By exercising, you can eliminate the physical side effects of stress while you take your mind off your troubles. If you do not usually exercise, take it slowly. Start with a 15-minute walk around the block or do some simple stretching exercises on the floor. Overdoing exercise can lead to more stress, so start small and increase the time you spend getting your blood circulating as you get stronger.

If you happen to exercise too much, you can look toward massage therapy to reduce your stress. Although it is a little less conventional than other methods of reducing stress, a massage can improve circulation and alleviate muscle soreness. You can seek professional massage therapy or ask a family member to rub your neck, shoulders, or feet. Massage therapy can give you the rejuvenation you need to tackle the rest of the week.

You have heard the cliché that "Laughter is the best medicine," and it is also an ideal way to eliminate stress. Have you ever been in a very stressful situation when someone made you laugh and you thought, "Boy, I needed that"? You probably felt all the tension melt away as you doubled over giggling. Surrounding yourself with people who make you laugh is one way to keep stress at a minimum. Other ways include renting comedies or reading funny books. Of course, good, old-fashioned acting silly can relieve stress and anxiety as well.

Last, you can comfort yourself with familiar favorites to eliminate the negative effects of stress. A special meal or a visit with your best friend can put you at ease. Looking at old photographs, reminiscing about family trips, and watching your favorite movies can be great stress relievers. If you have enrolled in college in a new town or you have moved out on your own for the first time, you may find comfort in the familiar, whether it is an old pillow or a favorite movie. Make sure, though, that your methods of reducing negative stress are healthy. Drugs and alcohol may temporarily relieve stress, but they cause more problems in the long run.

Reducing negative stress that you experience on the job, at home, and in college will be easier if the lines of communication are open and you are committed to explaining what is stressing you out. On the job, you may want to talk to your supervisor (rather than coworkers, unless they can truly help) about what is causing you stress and how you can manage it. You may find that your boss can reassure you that you are supported as you juggle both work and college. At home, you may want to talk with your family members about what stresses you out and why. Explain that your college career is temporary and that adjustments that need to be made at home will most likely be temporary until you complete your degree. If you are experiencing stress in college, speaking with a professor or a counselor can help you reduce the negative effects of stress. Remember that the people who work at a university were students, too, and may have some good tips that helped them minimize stress when they were in college.

G R I T
Instinct

Chances are you know people who deal with stress better than others. Ask yourself, "How would the grittiest, most resilient person I know deal with this situation?" Then give it a try!

Flexibility Can Help Minimize Stress

An important method of managing stress is to remain flexible. If you try to control too many aspects of your life, you will quickly discover you can't do it all. Although it is important to manage your time and mark your progress toward your goals, you still need to plan for the unexpected and be willing to make adjustments. Good time managers plan for problems by keeping their schedules loose enough to make room for adjustments. For example, if you have a doctor's appointment at 2:00, you shouldn't schedule a job interview at 3:00. Delays in the doctor's office or traffic problems could keep you from your 3:00 appointment and cause more stress. Instead, you should give yourself plenty of time in between scheduled tasks, especially if you will have to rely on others' time management skills. The idea is to build some margin in your life so you have a buffer to absorb the so-called "unexpected" events in our lives that we can actually expect. This margin can be in the form of time—giving yourself time to handle a traffic jam or a full parking lot to make it to class—or money—setting aside some money each month for an emergency fund to cover the flat tires, lost books, and parking tickets that always seem to come out of nowhere.

You can also build margins in your relationships by having some candid conversations with your friends, roommates, and loved ones about how you'll need their help and understanding when you're facing a lot of stress in your life. Simply forewarning your roommates that you have a challenging comprehensive exam next week can help them anticipate and effectively manage the situation if you seem more irritable or impatient than usual.

Seek Help for Your Stress If It Becomes Overwhelming

If you ever feel as though you cannot cope with the amount of work and responsibility that you have—despite attempts to reduce your stress—seek professional help. Excessive crying, difficulty breathing, inability to get out of bed, and suicidal thoughts are severe reactions to stress. Knowing when to reach out to other people will be crucial in your recovery.

When asking for help, find someone you trust and who will be objective about your experiences. Sometimes, close friends and family members can be your best allies to combat stress, but other times an outside party who will listen to what you have to say without judging can be extremely helpful. When you talk to someone, be honest about what you are feeling. Don't try to minimize any fear or anxiety. The more the person knows about what you are experiencing,

It's in the
syllabus

Use your syllabus to determine what you will need to be aware of during the semester so that you can better manage your stress.

- What parts of your professors' syllabi will cause you the most stress in terms of meeting the expectations?
- What will be easiest for you to meet?
- If you find yourself overwhelmed or confused by the expectations in your courses, what can you do to help eliminate your stress?

GRIT GAINER™

GIVE A SHOT OF GRIT   When an unexpected stress hits, immediately limit its negative impact by asking yourself, "How can I minimize the downside of this stress as quickly as possible?" A small dose of GRIT can contain a big dose of stress.

the better able he or she will be to help. Most universities have professional counselors with whom you can meet to share your experiences. They are professionally trained to help students navigate the stress and difficult emotional challenges that college students face, and they're on staff at the university to help you. Check with your health center or student affairs office if you can't locate contact information on the college website.

Your Physical Health Is Important

Your physical health directly affects your ability to perform well in college, and the habits you develop in college for maintaining your physical health will set the stage for your long-term health and well-being.

the unwritten rules
of Managing Stress

- **Everyone in college is under some kind of stress; they just handle it differently.** Students tend to think only about the stress they face, but the professors, staff members, and administrators on campus are also trying to manage stress. Everyone on campus has a shared responsibility to help each other manage stress and to try to avoid contributing to the stress that others experience.

- **Your choice of peers will dramatically affect how stressful your life is and how well you manage stress.** Face it—some people just seem to create more drama and stress than others. It might be funny and entertaining for a while, but after time it can wear on you and actually draw you into the stress. Steer clear of "drama queens" and "drama kings" and spend time with people who have healthy outlets for stress through laughing, exercising, and engaging in healthy and enjoyable recreational activities.

- **Maintaining good physical health in college requires more discipline than your earlier years.** You won't always feel like exercising, so there are times when you will have to just gut it out and go to the gym. You'll also be tempted to eat sugary snacks and drink sodas instead of a nutritious meal and a healthy beverage, but it's a matter of making good choices more often than you make poor ones. The reality is that your body becomes less forgiving of your poor choices as you get older.

- **We need to help each other.** If you see a friend or classmate clearly struggling, reach out to the person and support his or her efforts to get the help he or she needs. You don't have to be a counselor, just encourage and help the person get an appointment with a counselor. Wouldn't you want someone to do the same for you?

Nutrition Gives You Fuel

One key to living a healthy life is making it a priority to eat nutritious food. Getting the recommended daily allowances of fruits, vegetables, whole grains, proteins, and fats is a common-sense approach to healthy eating.

Eating healthy also means eating regularly. Most experts recommend eating smaller meals more frequently, rather than heavy meals five to seven hours apart. Start the day with a healthy breakfast, and you will feel more alert and energized throughout the morning. In addition to smaller, frequent nutritious meals, drinking plenty of water throughout the day has numerous health benefits, including regulating body temperature and assisting digestion. You should also consider drinking juices to get more nutrients.

© UWIMAGES/FOTOLIA

■ Making good food choices is the foundation for overall good health.

Exercise Gives You Energy and Relieves Stress

Regular exercise can lower blood pressure, increase your metabolism, improve muscle tone, and lessen your chances of suffering diseases that are directly related to a sedentary lifestyle. It can also improve your mood and your self-confidence. Doing 30 minutes of sustained activity three or four times a week will provide you with health benefits.

Resilience

Think of food as your climbing fuel, what you use to propel yourself forward and up along your ascent toward your goals. Would you put polluted fuel in your car, especially when it really needs to perform? Go for high-octane foods that optimize your focus and energy.

Sleep Recharges Your Batteries

Getting an adequate amount of sleep each night is as important to maintaining good health as what you eat and how often you exercise. Experts say that adults should get seven to nine hours of sleep a night to function normally throughout the day. Maintaining a regular schedule of going to bed and getting up will help you get the amount of sleep you need. Pulling all-nighters to study for tests or complete assignments is strongly discouraged, because it will make you less likely to perform well the next day.

Tenacity

Drugs and Alcohol Can Quickly Derail Your Health and Life

The more educated you become about the health risks that are associated with smoking and using smokeless tobacco, the more it will be obvious that using tobacco products can cause serious health consequences. There are a variety of methods for quitting;

Health clubs make their money off broken promises. They count on the majority of people who pay to sign up not showing up. It takes tenacity to stick to your promises and build your health. Think of yourself as an academic athlete, conditioning for the mountainous marathon required to get through, get out, and get paid.

it is worth investigating what your college and community offer if you are a smoker or a user of smokeless tobacco. Your college may provide information, support groups, or physician referrals for students who want to quit.

Alcohol and drugs are two other health issues that can dramatically affect college students. Whether they are consumed for recreational purposes or because of other, more serious health

Tenacity

reasons, abusing drugs and alcohol should not be a part of your college career because they will impede your achievement and potentially harm you and your loved ones.

In addition to abusing alcohol and illegal substances, using medications for purposes other than for what they were prescribed can have grave consequences, including death. Excessive use of medications that contain amphetamines and narcotics can lead to addiction and serious physical and emotional problems.

Lack of sleep saps your energy, effort, and GRIT. One of the secrets of high performers is that, no matter how busy they are, they make sleep sacred. Be tenacious about getting good-quality rest, so you can refuel your GRIT and your momentum.

Yes, We Do Need to Talk about Sex

A discussion of health issues would not be complete without talking about sexual health. Most colleges and universities strive to educate their students, especially those who are recently out of high school, about sexual responsibility, sexual assault, and common sexually transmitted diseases (STDs). Risky behavior, which includes having sex with multiple partners and having unprotected sex, opens the door to possible infections and illnesses such as chlamydia, gonorrhea, genital herpes, HIV, and AIDS. Some diseases can be transmitted in ways other than sexual intercourse. Hepatitis B and C are both diseases that can be contracted through shared razors, toothbrushes, body piercings, and tattooing.

Resilience

Drugs and alcohol are used to avoid adversity and stress, rather than deal with it. The stronger your GRIT, the less you need or even want drugs, excess alcohol, or any escapes. Instead, use life's daily stressors as fuel to stay challenged and engaged.

Sexual assaults in the university environment are a troubling phenomenon that you shouldn't ignore. Some of the most common incidents of sexual assault are related to excessive consumption of alcohol and date rape. The Rape, Abuse, and Incest National Network (RAINN) provides numerous resources that students can use to educate themselves about the risks, consequences, and preventative actions.

Instinct

Depression and Suicide Are Sad, but Real, Occurrences in College

A vital part of GRIT is listening to and honoring your instincts about what is right, good, smart, and healthy, and what is ultimately damaging, especially in the face of temptation. Be clear, strong, and unwavering on your most important goals, and be unwilling to do anything that can compromise your ability to get there.

Problems with depression often start before students enroll in college. Signs of depression include loss of pleasure in activities, feelings of hopelessness, inability to get out of bed, increased use of alcohol or drugs, changes in appetite or weight gain or loss, changes in sleep patterns (sleeping too little or too much), extreme sensitivity, excessive crying, lack of energy or interest in participating in activities, and lack of interest in taking care of oneself.

Suicide is another mental health issue that is associated with depression. Thoughts of ending your life should always be taken seriously and you should seek help immediately. Call a college counselor, an advisor, a hospital emergency room, or 911 if you are thinking about committing suicide. If one of your friends or roommates exhibits any behaviors or says anything that implies suicidal thoughts, do everything you can to put the person in contact with professionals on campus or at the local hospital who can help.

GRIT GAINER™

GET GRITTY FOR LONG-TERM HEALTH GRIT fuels health, and health fuels GRIT. Being a gritty student means making the right but often tough choices, and sacrificing short-term pleasures for your long-term goals. One way to really build your GRIT is to commit to and stay true to the right and best path forward.

THE G R I T ADVANTAGE

Upgrade your overall GRIT and your CORE response to any stress by asking one of these CORE Questions™:

Control: What are the facets of the situation I can potentially influence?

Ownership: How can I step up to improve this situation as quickly as possible?

Reach: What can I do to minimize the potential downside and maximize the potential upside of this situation?

Endurance: How can I get past this stressful situation as quickly as possible?

HOW GRITTY ARE YOU?

Now that you've completed this chapter, how committed are you to:

1. Owning your health, resilience, and how you respond to stressful events?

Zero Commitment 0 ———————————————— 10 **Fully Committed**

2. Digging deep and doing what it takes to remain healthy and strong?

Zero Commitment 0 ———————————————— 10 **Fully Committed**

3. Using your stress to motivate you to greater things?

Zero Commitment 0 ———————————————— 10 **Fully Committed**

12 Career Exploration

**Chapter goals
to help you**
get in,
get through,
get out,
and get paid:

We've used the phrase "get in, get through, get out, get paid," and in this chapter, we cover the last, most rewarding step in the process—getting paid!

**To meet
those goals,**
this chapter
will help you:

- Identify the tools and methods available for career exploration
- Develop an effective resume and cover letter
- Engage in networking activities that help you build important relationships
- Develop a plan for your life beyond college
- Appreciate and employ the **GRIT** edge for your career-related efforts

MyStudentSuccessLab

GRIT Log in to MyStudentSuccessLab.com to deepen your **GRIT** mindset and build the skills you'll need to get through the college experience.

Evan and Michael's Story

© MONKEY BUSINESS IMAGES/SHUTTERSTOCK

The big red arrow pointed to the ballroom. There were dozens of booths inviting students to leave their resumes and to learn more about a variety of businesses and industries.

In jeans and his university sweatshirt, Evan stopped to pick up a company brochure. "I'm planning on going to all the booths. Are you?" Evan asked.

Michael, wearing khakis and a white shirt, had done a little research and had already decided on the two booths he wanted to visit.

"No," he said. "I plan on finding the two companies I checked out on the Internet and leaving my resume."

"Aren't you afraid you will be cutting yourself short? Shouldn't you hit every one of the booths, just in case?" Evan asked.

"I think it is better to focus on one or two companies rather than all of them. Besides, I don't want just any job," Michael said.

Evan pulled out 30 copies of his resume from his backpack, walked to the first table, and introduced himself.

"I'm Evan. It is a pleasure to meet you," he said to the woman representing an aeronautics firm. "So, tell me what your company does and what I would do if I worked for you."

Michael walked straight to one of the two health care companies at the fair with his resume.

Now, what do you think?

- If you were unsure of what company you wanted to work for, how would you approach a career fair?
  a. Focus more on how companies are trying to recruit me rather than how I can impress them
  b. Be selective and do my research before I attend
  c. Be open to all the possibilities by going to every employer—you never know what you may like or who may like you

- How would you introduce yourself to a potential employer?
  a. Provide a general resume that would fit any job and say that I am interested in all jobs
  b. Tell the employer that I want to be the CEO in two years so that I impress them with my ambition
  c. Explain what I know about the company, the open position, and how I am qualified for the job

Your Career Starts Here

Whether you know exactly what career you want or you are still exploring the possibilities, your college experience can help you focus on what you want out of your professional life. Although it may seem like your career won't start until you're done with college, the exciting reality is that the decisions you are making today are already starting to form your career. College is the time for exploring and preparing for a career, and the first step is to know your goals and values.

Growth

Smart isn't enough. New research shows employers put a premium on GRIT. The tougher the challenges and obstacles you face, and the more difficult path you take, the more attractive you will be. The choices you make now will show up in your resume and job interviews later.

Career Values and Goals Set the Course for Your Journey

Before you begin delving into the resources and services available at your college, take some time to reflect on what your career values and goals are. Values are personal and professional qualities and principles that are deeply important to you. For example, you may have a passionate interest in working for a company that has a positive social or environmental impact. Or, it may be critically important to you to work for an organization that is honest and ethical.

In addition to considering your values as they relate to your career, you may also want to consider what your goals are. Goals are tangible outcomes that you want to achieve in your personal and professional lives. For example, is one of your goals to move

Tenacity

A Gallup poll of 25 million people shows 70 percent of working people are disengaged, meaning they are not excited about what they are doing and not giving their best. Those who have jobs with the most alignment with their values and goals and those with the greatest GRIT are the most engaged. They *enjoy* their work.

up quickly in a company or to find a business that will allow you to travel and meet a diverse group of people? When you get to the point that you will be creating clear, realistic, and reachable career goals, they will be influenced by your values. Your values and goals will also help you with talking with a career counselor, searching for a job, and interviewing.

Different Careers Mean Different Experiences

In addition to your personal values and goals, it is worth considering what you value in a career and what kinds of experiences you want to have. For example, do you value working with others in projects with strict deadlines or would you prefer to work alone with little supervision? Your answer to that question and others can help you determine what you value and what careers work best for you. If, for instance, you have a strong interest in writing, but you prefer working with others, you may decide to choose a career that has many opportunities for collaboration when writing.

If you are not sure where to start when considering your career values and goals, then you may want to check out the various career assessment programs, such as DISCOVER or Kuder, at your career counseling center. There are also a number of websites and books, such as Richard N. Bolles's *What Color Is Your Parachute?* (2011), that offer helpful guidance for identifying your career interests, even at the early stages of your college career.

The career landscape can seem daunting and complex, especially because technology seems to cause careers to change so quickly. Careers that existed 10 years ago may not exist four years from now, and careers that didn't exist a few years ago are now emerging. For that reason, don't put pressure on yourself to identify a specific company and job title for your career goal. Instead, keep your focus on the kind of career you want to have in terms of its general characteristics—work environment, industry, technical requirements, individual versus team environment, highly structured versus unstructured organizational structure and job functions, and the like. Take time to browse career listings on websites such as careerbuilder.com and save a copy of the posts that capture your interest. These will help you paint a picture that captures both your values and goals as they emerge and develop over time. It's OK if your interests change over time; this will happen as you take more classes and gain new perspective from your college experience. In fact, in today's work environment, the average individual will have several careers over her lifetime. What you're developing in college is the ability to identify your interests and abilities and match them with the career opportunities in the marketplace. You may not want to face this reality now, but you may very well find yourself back in college later in your life to pursue an advanced degree or certificate or a second bachelor's degree as you recreate yourself throughout your lifetime. As you learn to use the tools and resources we'll discuss in this next section, you'll be encouraged to know that they can serve you well throughout your career journey.

GRIT
Growth

The job world is changing so fast that many of the most exciting jobs you might want to consider when you graduate don't even exist today. They aren't on the standard menu. Show some GRIT by asking anyone who looks like he enjoys his work or whose life you admire about what he does and what he would suggest you consider.

Meeting
expectations

The college will expect that I . . .	To meet that expectation, I will . . .
Example: . . . know what career I want to pursue when I graduate.	*Example:* . . . explore my options and take a proactive role to determine which careers would be best for me.
_____	_____
_____	_____
_____	_____

There Are Several Ways to Explore Your Career

There are several resources and events on your campus to support your efforts to explore and pursue your career options and opportunities. These include career counselors and professors, career fairs, and internships.

Career Counselors Can Be Your Best Supporters

Even though you won't pursue a full-time career until you graduate, commit yourself to meeting with a counselor your freshman year so you can put an effective plan in place for both internships and your career. Each college offers different services in its career center, but most provide access to interest inventories and resources on different careers, which can help you pinpoint which careers you are best suited for. In addition, career centers

© APOPS/FOTOLIA

■ Use events and people on campus as opportunities to help you build a professional network.

may offer help with writing a cover letter and resume and tips for interviewing for a job. Evan should spend some time in his college's career library to learn more about careers before he hits all of the employers at the career fair.

Don't forget that your professors can also be great career counselors because they often have connections with people in the field (or have friends or relatives working in different industries). You never know when your sociology professor may have a contact at an accounting firm or a biology professor may have a connection with the human resources department at an advertising firm. Tell professors what you want to do as a career whenever you have a chance. They may remember you and your goals when they meet someone in your field of study.

Internships Give You and Your Employer a Chance for a Test Drive

Another work option for college students is an internship. This is a supervised position that allows a student to work for an organization before they graduate. Some internships are unpaid, which makes them less attractive to students who need to work. However, you may be able to earn academic credit for a paid or unpaid internship, so check with your advisor well in advance about this possibility. Internships are a great way to make progress toward your degree and to explore careers. Another idea is to volunteer once or twice a week at a place of business. If you have a few extra hours a week or can trade college credit for an internship, then you should investigate the benefits of interning.

Why are internships such a good opportunity for college students? One reason is that they allow you to work closely in a field that you may be interested in. In addition, internships can help you explore different ways that a major can be used in the workforce. For example, an English or journalism major may want to participate in an internship at a newspaper or as a technical editor at a company. A computer science major may want to intern at a small business to get practical experience with computer networking issues. These opportunities can give you firsthand experience with using what you're learning in your degree.

It's in the
syllabus

Your syllabus may help you in your career exploration. Look at what you are covering during the semester.

● Do any topics really interest you?

● Do you find yourself drawn to certain subjects? What are they?

● Which instructors do you have now who will be helpful to you in the future?

Internships also allow you to network with others who can help you find a job once you graduate. Even if you decide that you don't want to work in the same area as your internship, you will have contacts who may help you find a job in other fields. If you decide to intern, you should treat it as a career. Some employers rely on interns to complete certain projects each year, and they will expect that you be serious about the position, even if you don't get paid. Keeping a good attitude and being self-motivated are excellent ways to shine during your internship. In addition, you should meet regularly with your supervisor to ask questions and get guidance on projects. Most of all, make the best of your unique opportunity and add that experience to your resume.

Networking Opens Doors for Your Career

Networking is developing relationships and contacts with people now who may, sometime in the future, prove to be helpful to you in pursuing your goals. Now, more than ever, networking is an essential part of an effective career search. If you ask 10 recent college graduates who have full-time careers how they landed their jobs, chances are that at least six of them will tell a story about how someone they knew helped them meet someone in the organization to get a first interview. If you establish good relationships with a variety of individuals across multiple companies and industries throughout your college experience—including your freshman year—these individuals will be your primary gateway to those initial interviews.

It's important to establish what networking can and cannot do for your career search. Effective networking throughout your college years can help you get your foot in the door at various organizations, and may help you land that first interview. At that point, however, it's all up to you. Someone else's referral on your behalf is often enough for a recruiter to take time to give you an interview, but it's not enough for her to hire you. You have to prove yourself in the interview process and, once you're hired, you have to prove yourself on the job. In a competitive job market in which hundreds of people are applying for a single position, landing that first interview is a crucial step, and networking can help you get there.

Practice interviewing with a fellow student or a career counselor before going out there for real.

© RUBBERBALL PRODUCTIONS/GETTY IMAGES

Networking Is More Than Exchanging Business Cards

When you see the word *networking,* what scene or activities do you picture in your mind? The stereotypical perception of networking is a bunch of people introducing themselves to each other and chatting at a social or business function. Some people think they've done a good job of networking if they came home from an event with a lot of business cards in their pockets. However, networking is a lot more than that. It certainly begins with an initial point of contact, and for that you need to make a professional first impression. How you dress, what you say, and how you act during the initial social exchange will be important. But once you've made that initial contact with someone, how you follow up and maintain contact really determines the value of your network.

Let's say that you're at a relative's wedding and you meet someone who has a highly successful career at an accounting firm. At the time, you have no interest in accounting, nor do you know much about the company he works for, but you take time to ask questions about his career and organization, and you politely ask him for his business card or contact information. Was that networking? Yes, but you're just getting started. It's what happens after the introduction that matters most. When you get home, you need to add that person's contact information to a database, then compose a follow-up email or personal letter expressing your sentiments that you enjoyed meeting him and learning about his career and that you'd like to stay in touch with him as your college career progresses. If you have a current resume prepared, you could send that to him, even if you don't have a present interest in a career at his organization.

Instinct

In the months and years to follow, you can use a calendar system to remind yourself to touch base with that person. You can update him on your accomplishments in college, ask him about his career accomplishments, ask him questions about how he chose his career, arrange an informational interview at his firm, and share any news articles that you read that have something to do with his industry or company. As you invest

> People love to be asked for advice. A gritty way to get what you want is to sincerely ask people for their advice on who or what you should pursue and how best to go at it.

in this relationship over time, you're building a connection. Then, when you really need the individuals in your network to help you secure that first interview, they know you well enough to trust in your personal qualities and professionalism.

When someone takes the risk of recommending you to one of his friends or associates for a job interview, he is putting his own reputation at risk on your behalf. This is a significant request! Successful networking—over time—establishes a range of personal and professional relationships that can help you make the right connection at the right time when your career search gets into full swing. If you wait until late in your college career to start networking, it will be far more difficult for you to prove your sincerity and professionalism through the test of time. Start early and build a broad network, because you never know where your interests may take you in the future.

Networking Face to Face

The most effective method of networking is by building relationships through face-to-face interactions. There are a number of specific activities you can pursue that will help you form broad, long-term connections:

- Look to clubs on campus that share your interests. Even if they are not career-related, such as a drama club, you will meet people who may be future contacts for jobs.

- Scan your school newspaper and announcements for events, such as guest speakers and discussion panels. Colleges often host influential experts or industry leaders for speaking engagements. Attend these events when you can, not only to learn new perspectives, but also in an effort to meet these individuals and introduce yourself.

- Join a college ambassador club or other host-related student organization. Many colleges have a student ambassador group that plays a lead role in hosting distinguished college guests, provides campus tours for visitors, and represents the college at community events, such as Chamber of Commerce meetings and special task forces and committees.

- Consider a student leadership position on your campus. Student leaders, such as the members of the student council, often have special access to college administrators and community leaders.

Tenacity

- Get involved in community service and philanthropic activities. Industry and community leaders—the kinds of people who are ideal to have in your personal network—are often actively engaged in nonprofit organizations, community service activities, and philanthropy. You probably wouldn't bump into the CEO of a large organization in your daily life as a college student, but if you invest yourself in community service and philanthropy, you might find yourself working next to someone who could eventually become a valuable member of your network.

> Gritty students don't just sign up, they show up. And they contribute. They do the hard part, which is investing their time, effort, and energy into helping others, in whatever organizations they sign up for. Employers can spot the difference between "resume padders" and real contributors.

the unwritten rules
about Career Planning

- **The early bird gets the worm.** Those who are the first to pursue an opportunity have a better chance of seizing it. This holds true for your career pursuits. If you're proactive and earlier than your peers in developing a resume, building a network, and applying for internships, you're giving yourself a better chance of securing a good job while you're in college and after graduating.

- **The best careers come from where you least expect them.** While serving as a restaurant waiter or hostess, you might serve a client who turns out to be a major employer, recruiter, or entrepreneur. By demonstrating some interest in that person and listening well, you could pick up clues that open the door for you to introduce yourself and express interest in his company. Be ready to give your 30-second elevator pitch at any time, even in the bathroom!

- **Students can have business cards, too.** If you have access to a computer, you have what you need to design and print a professional-looking business card. Include your name, the university you attend, your major, and your contact information, and have some of these cards available at all times.

- **Eportfolios are coming.** An eportfolio is a website where students compile a carefully selected sample of their academic work and accomplishments to show to prospective employers or graduate schools. Increasingly, employers want to see more than just a resume—they want to see samples of your actual work, including papers you've written, computer programs you've developed, projects you've completed, and problems you've solved. If you start collecting and organizing your work immediately during your first term, you'll have a lot more content to use for an eportfolio when you're ready to build it.

As you pursue these networking opportunities, it's important that you carry them out with a genuine interest in making a contribution to these organizations and that you aren't simply participating just to meet people. Before you commit to any club, organization, community event, or philanthropic cause, be sure that it's something you really believe in and are willing to support. Otherwise, your lack of sincerity and commitment will hurt your reputation, and you'll do more harm than good. However, if you get involved in something that you really believe in and support, the personal network of relationships you establish will open doors for you in your career that you never could have imagined for yourself.

GRIT GAINER™

GRITTY GO-GETTERS GRIT is the most powerful weapon you have in winning the job wars. Many people who have the most exciting and fulfilling careers were turned down, often multiple times. They were told "no," but they used their GRIT to help achieve a "yes" on the things that count.

integrity matters

Although you may be excited to include your accomplishments on your resume, you will need to be sure that you do not go overboard. A good rule to follow is to always provide accurate, truthful information in your resume and cover letter. Highlight your accomplishments without exaggerating them.

Lying on a resume is called *resume padding*, and it can get you in serious trouble. At the very least, you may not get the job; at the very worst, you could be fired after you are hired if the company finds out that your resume contains false information.

YOUR TURN

In approximately 250 words, describe where you think the line exists between making your accomplishments noteworthy and exaggerating them. Discuss what steps you will take to ensure that all of your information for a resume or a cover letter is accurate.

Networking Online

One of the largest trends in networking is using social networking websites, such as Linked In and Facebook, to create networks of friends, family, and special interest groups. The possibilities seem endless as to how you can use the Internet to connect with others. With this said, if you decide to join a network that focuses on an interest of yours, such as computer programming, be sure to investigate who runs the group, what kinds of information are shared, and how active the group is. Some networks will be more active than others, which will make it easier to connect with others and get involved; other networks or groups may be less active, which won't help you if you are using them to get to know others as potential contacts in the future. Because creating networks of your own is so easy, you may want to consider creating a group if you cannot find one relating to your career of interest. Networking sites such as Facebook allow you to set up groups that can be used for professional, educational, or social purposes.

If you decide to set up a profile on a social network site like LinkedIn, take time to establish a profile that is well written, professional, and informative. These sites often allow you to post a photo, so provide one that shows you dressed professionally, as you would appear for a job interview. Upload your resume and make sure that all of your contact information is current, accurate, and professional. These types of sites often have a mechanism for you to connect with others, and in most cases this requires the other person to accept your invitation. Be sure to initiate these invitations with a courteous, respectful approach, recognizing that if they choose to connect with you, it's comparable to the risk they face when recommending you to others. This is not a trivial decision on someone's part, so be sure that your profile and your request are presented in a manner that gives the person confidence that you will represent yourself—and the person's reputation—well.

Your Resume Establishes Your Personal Brand

As you progress through your degree, your resume and cover letter will serve as a tangible representation of your personal brand—who you are, what you know, what you can do, and how you're different from your peers and other individuals competing for the same jobs. Just as McDonald's, Apple, and the Gap invest significant effort and resources to define themselves through a distinctive brand, you also need to establish a distinctive personal brand that makes

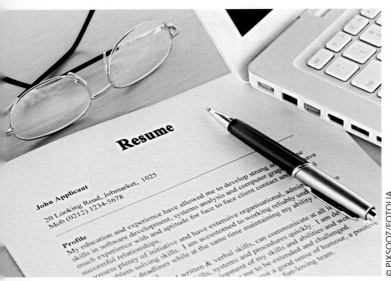

■ Creating a strong, compelling resume can be the difference between getting an interview and getting overlooked.

you recognizable and relevant to organizations who need a talented workforce. If you'd like to learn more about developing your personal brand, Tim O'Brien's book *The Power of Personal Branding* (2007) is a great resource (www. thepersonalbrandinggroup.com).

Your Resume Puts Your Life on Paper

Learning to write a resume is an essential skill for new graduates, and there is no time like the present to begin honing that skill. A resume is no place to be modest, but neither is it a place to embellish or misrepresent your skills or experience. Everyone has something—whether it's the classes they've taken, the projects they've completed, or the hardships they've overcome in their personal life—that makes them special and gives them experience and personal qualities that are important to an employer. The challenge is to describe these qualities in no more than a page.

There are a number of university-affiliated websites that provide guidance for how to develop an effective resume, and your university's career services office will offer support resources as well. To get you started, here's an initial list of what your resume should include:

- **Your name and contact information, including your address, phone number, and email address.** Make sure your voicemail has an appropriate message on it, and that your email is professional as well: ejcantu@abcmail.com is preferred over bananafreak72@chunkymonkey.com.

- **A clear objective or purpose statement that describes your career goals.** Objectives are not always written in a complete sentence. You may want to develop versions of your resume with different purpose statements so that you can personalize what you send to different companies in different industries.

- **Information about your educational accomplishments.** If you have not completed your degree at this point, you can write down the anticipated date: "Bachelor of Arts, May 2016." Be sure to include any other certificates or degrees that you have earned.

- **Information about your work history.** Again, list your most recent job first and include the dates you worked, your position title, the name of the company and location, and a bulleted list of job responsibilities, written with action verbs such as *organized, developed, implemented,* and *managed.*

- **Extracurricular activities, organizations, or awards.** If you received a college scholarship, volunteer regularly with your child's school, participated in a fundraising event, organized a community meeting, coached a sport, or sat on a committee at your church or synagogue, list these activities to demonstrate your accomplishments and contributions to society. Also, be sure to list college-related accomplishments like dean's list or participation in student government and organizations.

- **A list of references.** As you meet people in college, you may want to create a list of potential references. A professor whom you got to know well, your advisor whom you see each semester as you plan your degree, or a campus official with whom you have worked closely on a project are good candidates for letters of recommendation or references. People you have worked with—either on the job or through a community project—are other excellent possibilities for references. Getting their permission before you list them is essential to getting a good reference.

A cover letter accompanies a resume and explains in detail how your qualifications match what the employer is looking for. As with a resume, keep a cover letter brief and to the point, usually no more than a page. The more concise your resume and cover letter, the easier it will be for potential employers to determine whether you are right for the job.

Instinct

As you consider what content to include in your resume, think of it as body of evidence to support every claim you would want to make about yourself in an interview. If you believe that you are a hardworking person, then your resume might illustrate how you've managed to work during college. If you're an effective communicator, the resume itself should be well written, and you could reference the high grades you've received in your composition and technical writing classes or that you've participated on a high school debate team.

> A ground-breaking study looked at 30,000 resumes to figure out what, if any, factors made the difference on who gets the job and who doesn't. The resumes that had a statement communicating GRIT—a tough goal they took on and achieved against daunting odds—had *triple* the chance of getting the job.

THE GRIT ADVANTAGE

You can enhance your GRIT game now by asking yourself these questions:

1. What challenge can you take on now that would demonstrate your GRIT and enhance your career prospects?

2. What is your best adversity story? What is the greatest challenge or obstacle you have had to successfully navigate to achieve positive results in your life?

3. List five people you most admire and from whom you would most want advice on how to have not just good, but *great,* career options.

4. What community or group can you join that would be the most likely to challenge and improve you as a human being?

HOW GRITTY ARE YOU?

Now that you've completed this chapter, how committed are you to:

1. Doing things that use and prove your GRIT so you are more attractive and valuable to future employers?

   Zero Commitment 0 ————————————————————————— 10 Fully Committed

2. Owning and relentlessly building your own career prospects by tapping the available resources and asking the right people for their advice?

   Zero Commitment 0 ————————————————————————— 10 Fully Committed

3. Striving to clarify your values, goals, and mission and then pursuing a career where you can bring them to life?

   Zero Commitment 0 ————————————————————————— 10 Fully Committed

Glossary

Academic calendar—A list of important dates. Included are vacation breaks, registration periods, and deadlines for certain forms.

Academic probation—A student whose GPA falls below a designated number can be placed on academic probation. If the GPA does not improve, then the student may be prohibited from registering for classes for a designated number of semesters.

Adjunct instructor—An instructor who is not employed full-time with the college. An adjunct instructor usually teaches one or two courses at the college.

Articulation agreement—A signed document stating that one college will accept the courses from another college.

Asynchronous communication—When two or more people do not have to be communicating at the same time. Email and discussion boards are asynchronous communication methods.

Audience—In essay writing, the audience is the person or persons whom you are addressing.

Bursar—The person at your college who handles payments for tuition and fees.

Chat room—An electronic method of communicating with other people in real time.

Corequisite—A course that you can take at the same time as another course. For example, if intermediate algebra is a corequisite for physical science, then you will take both courses during the same semester.

Cornell System—A note-taking system in which a student draws an upside-down "T" on a sheet of paper and uses the space to the right for taking notes, the space to the left for adding questions and highlighting important points, and the space at the bottom for summarizing the material.

Course catalog—A book that provides students with information about the college's academic calendar, tuition and fees, and degree/certificate programs.

Course objective—A goal that the instructor has identified for the student to meet once the course is completed. For example, a course objective could be to use MLA documentation properly.

Cover letter—A letter accompanying a resume that describes how a person's qualifications match the advertised requirements for the job.

Critical thinking—The ability to use specific criteria to evaluate reasoning and make a decision.

Curriculum—A term used to refer to the courses that a student must take in a particular field, or it can refer to all the classes that the college offers.

Dean—An administrator who is in charge of faculty or a division in the college.

Developmental classes—Sometimes referred to as *remedial classes*, developmental classes focus on basic college-level skills such as reading, writing, and math. Students who earn a certain score on standardized tests such as the ACT and COMPASS exams may be required to take developmental classes before enrolling in college-level courses.

Discussion board—An electronic method of interacting with other people by posting messages and reading postings from other people.

Family Educational Rights and Privacy Act (FERPA)—A federal law that ensures that a student's educational records, including test grades and transcripts, are not accessed or viewed by anyone who is not authorized to do so.

Full-time student—A student who is taking at least 12 credit hours of courses per semester.

Full-time worker—A person who is working at least 40 hours per week.

Grade point average (GPA)—The number that is used to determine a student's progress in college. It refers to the number of quality points divided by the number of hours a student has taken.

GRIT—Your capacity to dig deep and do whatever it takes—even sacrifice, struggle, and suffer—in the pursuit of your most important goals.

Growth—Your tendency to seek fresh angles on situations and to view success as a matter of effort, more than talent or smarts.

Information literacy—A set of abilities requiring an individual to determine when information is needed, locate appropriate information for the need, assess the information as to accuracy and relevancy, and use the information in an ethical manner.

Instinct—Your gut-level capacity to pursue the right goals in the most efficient and effective ways.

Knowledge—This comes from taking in information, thinking about it critically, and synthesizing one's own ideas about what one has read or seen.

Long-term goal—A goal that takes a long time to complete (within a year or more).

Major—The area that a student is focusing on for his or her degree. If a student wants to teach third grade, his or her major can be elementary education. (*See also* Minor.)

Matching question—A test question that provides one column of descriptors and another column of words that must be matched with the appropriate descriptor.

Minor—A second area that a student can emphasize in his or her degree. A minor usually requires fewer classes and is not as intensive as a major. For example, if a student majors in marketing but also wants to learn more about running his or her own business, the student may want to minor in business or accounting.

Mission statement—A declaration of what a person or an institution believes in and what that person or institution hopes to accomplish.

Multiple-choice question—A type of test question in which an incomplete sentence or a question is given and the correct response must be chosen from a list of possibilities.

Objective question—A question that presents a limited number of possible answers.

OK5R—A reading strategy developed by Dr. Walter Pauk that stands for Overview, Key Ideas, Read, Record, Recite, Review, and Reflect.

Part-time student—A student who is taking less than 12 credit hours per semester.

Prerequisite—A required course or score that must be completed or achieved before enrolling in a course.

Priority—Something that is important at that moment.

Provost—A high-ranking college administrator.

Purpose—What a student hopes to accomplish with his or her writing assignment.

Quality points—The number that is assigned to each grade. For example, an A is worth four quality points and a B is worth three quality points.

Registrar—The official record keeper at the college.

Remedial classes—*See* Developmental classes.

Resilience—Your capacity to respond constructively to, and make good use of, tough moments, including all kinds of difficulty, adversity, and challenges.

Resume—A page or two that provides a person's educational and work experience, career objective, and contact information.

Short-term goal—A goal that can be accomplished in a short period of time (within a week or a few months).

Stress—A physical and psychological response to outside stimuli.

Student handbook—A publication of the college that outlines what the college expects of the student.

Subjective question—A test question that requires a student to provide a personal answer. Usually, there are no "wrong" answers to subjective questions.

Syllabus—A document that contains an overview of the course, including objectives, assignments, and required materials as well as the instructor's policies for attendance, exams, and grading. It may also contain the college's policies on disability accommodations and academic dishonesty.

Synchronous communication—When two or more people have to be communicating at the same time. Internet-based synchronous communication includes chat rooms.

Tenacity—Your sheer persistence; the degree to which you commit to, stick with, and relentlessly work at whatever you choose.

Time management—Strategies for using time effectively.

Topic—The subject of a piece of writing.

Transcript—A record of the courses a student has taken and the grades the student has earned. Transcripts also note the student's grade point average.

Transfer—Refers to moving from one school to another. Students who transfer must apply for admissions to the second school and must request that their transcript(s) be sent to the new school.

T-System—*See* Cornell System.

Values—Part of a person's belief system that provides the foundation of what the person does and what the person wants to become. If a person values financial stability, then the person will look for opportunities to earn money and provide a secure future.

Work-study—A federal program that allows students to work at their college while taking classes. Students must qualify for work-study money and must meet college department requirements for work.

References and Recommended Readings

Chapter 1

Banner, J. M., & Cannon, H. C. (1999). *The elements of learning*. New Haven, CT: Yale University Press.

The College Board. (2008). *Succeeding in college: What it means and how to make it happen*. Plano, TX: College Board.

Dabbah, M. (2009). *Latinos in college: Your guide to success*. Scarborough, NY: Consultare.

Newport, C. (2005). *How to win at college: Surprising secrets for success from the country's top students*. New York, NY: Broadway.

Nist-Olejnik, S., & Patrick Holschuh, J. (2007). *College rules! How to study, survive, and succeed in college*. Berkeley, CA: Ten Speed Press.

Stoltz, P. G. (1999). *The adversity quotient: Turning obstacles into opportunities*. New York, NY: Wiley.

Watkins, B. D. (2004). *Everything you ever wanted to know about college: A guide for minority students*. Camillus, NY: Blue Boy Publishing.

Chapter 2

Beals, M. P. (1994). *Warriors don't cry*. New York, NY: Pocket Books.

Dickerson, D. J. (2000). *An American story*. New York, NY: Anchor Books.

Lazear, D. (1991). *Seven ways of teaching: The artistry of teaching with multiple intelligences*. Palatine, IL: Skylight Publishing.

Myers-Briggs Type Indicator. (2009). Retrieved September 22, 2014, from www.myersbriggstypeindicator.co.uk

Rodriguez, R. (1982). *Hunger of memory: The education of Richard Rodriguez*. New York, NY: The Dial Press.

Smiley, T. (2006). *What I know for sure: My story of growing up in America*. New York, NY: Anchor Books.

Chapter 3

Gurin, P. (1999). New research on the benefits of diversity in college and beyond: An empirical analysis. Retrieved July 11, 2011, from www.diversityweb.org/digest/sp99/benefits.html

Katz, N. (2005). Sexual harassment statistics in the workplace and in education. Retrieved July 5, 2005, from http://womenissues.about.com/cs/sexdiscrimination/a/sexharassstats.htm

Zemke, R., Raines, C., & Filipczak, B. (2000). *Generations at work: Managing the clash of veterans, boomers, xers, and nexters in your workplace*. New York, NY: Amacom.

Chapter 4

Allen, D., Schwartz, T., & McGinn, D. (2011). Being more productive. *Harvard Business Review, 89*(5), 82–88.

Dodd, P., & Sundheim, D. (2005). *The 25 best time management tools and techniques: How to get more done without driving yourself crazy*. Chelsea, MI: Peak Performance Press.

Hindle, T. (1998). *Manage your time*. New York, NY: DK Publishing.

Leland, K., & Bailey, K. (2008). *Time management in an instant: 60 ways to make the most of your day*. Franklin Lakes, NJ: The Career Press.

Nelson, D. B., & Low, G. R. (2003). *Emotional intelligence: Achieving academic and career excellence*. Upper Saddle River, NJ: Pearson.

Schwartz, T. (2007). Manage your energy, not your time. *Harvard Business Review, 85*(10), 63–70.

Sibler, L. (1998). *Time management for the creative person: Right-brain strategies for stopping procrastination, getting control of the clock and calendar, and freeing up your time and your life*. New York, NY: Three Rivers Press.

Tyson, D. (2009). *Personal finance for dummies* (6th ed.). New York, NY: Wiley.

Chapter 5

American Heart Association. (2009). Cigarette smoking statistics. Retrieved September 6, 2009, from www.americanheart.org/presenter.jhtml?identifier=4559

Gately, G. (2003, August 23). College students ignoring risks of unprotected sex. *Health Day News*. Retrieved August 29, 2005, from www.hon.ch/News/HSN/514968.html

Mayo Clinic. Interval training: Can it boost your calorie-burning power? Retrieved July 19, 2011, from www.mayoclinic.com/health/interval-training/SM00110

RAINN. (2014). Reducing your risk of sexual assault. Retrieved September 22, 2014, from https://rainn.org/get-information/sexual-assault-prevention

U.S. Food and Drug Administration. (2014). How to understand and use the nutrition facts label. Retrieved September 22, 2014, from www.fda.gov/Food/IngredientsPackagingLabeling/LabelingNutrition/ucm274593.htm

Chapter 6

Diestler, S. (1998). *Becoming a critical thinker: A user friendly manual* (2nd ed.). Upper Saddle River, NJ: Prentice Hall.

Dweck, C. (2006). *Mindset: The new psychology of success.* New York, NY: Random House.

Foer, J. (2007). Remember this. *National Geographic, 212*(5), 32–55.

Gunn, A. M., Richburg, R. W., & Smilkstein, R. (2007). *Igniting student potential: Teaching with the brain's natural learning process.* Thousand Oaks, CA: Corwin Press.

Harris, R. (2002). *Creative problem solving: A step-by-step approach.* Los Angeles, CA: Pyrczak.

Miller, G. (1956). The magical number seven, plus or minus two: Some limits on our capacity for processing information. Retrieved July 5, 2011, from www.musanim.com/miller1956/

Chapter 7

International Dyslexia Association. (2007). IDA fact sheets on dyslexia and related language-based learning disabilities. Retrieved September 22, 2014, from www.interdys.org

Orfalea, P., & Marsh, A. (2007). *Copy this! Lessons from a hyperactive dyslexic who turned a bright idea into one of America's best companies.* New York, NY: Workman.

Robinson, F. P. (1970). *Effective study* (4th ed.). New York, NY: Harper & Row.

Chapter 8

Beglar, D., & Murray, N. (2009). *Contemporary topics 3: Academic and note-taking skills* (3rd ed.). Boston, MA: Pearson.

Kline, J. A. (1996). *Effective listening.* Maxwell Air Force Base, AL: Air University Press.

Rowson, P. (2007). *Communicating with more confidence: The easy step-by-step guide* (Rev. ed.). Hayling, England: Summersdale Publishers.

Spears, D. (2008). *Developing critical reading skills.* New York, NY: McGraw-Hill.

Chapter 9

Bradbury, A. (2006). *Successful presentation skills* (3rd ed.). London, UK: Kogan Page.

Tracy, B. (2008). *Speak to win: How to present with power in any situation.* New York, NY: AMACOM Books.

Strunk, W., & White, E. B. (2008). *The elements of style* (50th anniv. ed.). New York, NY: Longman.

Wilder, L. (1999). *Seven steps to fearless speaking.* New York, NY: Wiley.

Zinsser, W. (2006). *On writing well* (30th anniv. ed.). New York, NY: Harper Paperbacks.

Chapter 10

Paul, M. A., & Paul, K. (2009). *Study smarter, not harder.* Bellingham, WA: Self Counsel Press.

Roubidoux, S. (2008). *101 ways to make studying easier and faster for college students: What every student needs to know explained simply.* Ocala, FL: Atlantic Publishing Group.

Chapter 11

The College Board. (2009). *Getting financial aid 2010.* New York, NY: The College Board.

Cress, C. M., Collier, P. J., & Reitenauer, V. L. (2005). *Learning through serving: A student guidebook for service-learning across the disciplines.* Sterling, VA: Stylus.

Lipphardt, D. (2008). *The scholarship and financial aid solution: How to go to college for next to nothing with short cuts, tricks, and tips from start to finish.* Ocala, FL: Atlantic Publishing Group.

Schlacther, G., & Weber, R. D. (2009). *Kaplan Scholarships 2010: Billions of dollars in free money for college.* Fort Lauderdale, FL: Kaplan Publishing.

Perkins Loans. (2011). *Student aid on the web.* Retrieved July 11, 2011, from http://studentaid.ed.gov/PORTALSWebApp/students/english/campusaid.jsp

U.S. Department of Education. (2011). Types of federal student aid. Retrieved July 11, 2011, from http://studentaid.ed.gov/students/publications/student_guide/2006-2007/english/typesofFSA_grants.htm

U.S. Department of Veterans Affairs. (2011). What is the Post-9/11 G.I. Bill? Retrieved July 11, 2011, from www.gibill.va.gov/benefits/post_911_gibill/index.html

Chapter 12

The College Board. (2013). *Education pays 2013: The benefits of higher education for individuals and society.* New York, NY: The College Board.

Farr, M. J. (2004). *Same-day résumé: Write an effective résumé in an hour.* Indianapolis, IN: Jist Publishing.

Leider, R. J. (2005). *The power of purpose: Creating meaning in your life and work.* San Francisco: Berrett-Koehler Publishers.

Leonhardt. (2014). "Is college worth it? Clearly, new data say." *New York Times,* www.nytimes.com/2014/05/27/upshot/is-college-worth-it-clearly-new-data-say.html?smid=tw-share&_r=0

Marcus, J. J. (2003). *The résumé makeover: 50 common résumé and cover letter problems—and how to fix them.* New York, NY: McGraw-Hill.

Pew Research Center. (2014). "The rising cost of not going to college." www.pewsocialtrends.org/files/2014/02/SDT-higher-ed-FINAL-02-11-2014.pdf

Safko, L., & Brake, D. (2009). *The social media bible: Tactics, tools, and strategies for business success.* Hoboken, NJ: Wiley & Sons.

Shellenbarger, S. (2009, Dec. 16). "Weighing the value of that college diploma." *Wall Street Journal,* p. D1.

Index